ESSENTIALS OF
TRANSDISCIPLINARY RESEARCH

Qualitative Essentials

Series Editor:
Janice Morse, *University of Utah*

Qualitative Essentials is a book series providing a comprehensive but succinct overview of topics in qualitative inquiry. These books will fill an important niche in qualitative methods for students—and others new to the qualitative research—who require rapid but complete perspective on specific methods, strategies, and important topics. Written by leaders in qualitative inquiry, alone or in combination, these books are an excellent resource for instructors and students from all disciplines. Proposals for the series should be sent to the series editor at explore@lcoastpress.com.

Titles in this series:

ESSENTIALS OF TRANSDISCIPLINARY RESEARCH

Using Problem-Centered Methodologies

Patricia Leavy

Left Coast
Press Inc.

Walnut Creek, California

Left Coast Press Inc.

LEFT COAST PRESS, INC.
1630 North Main Street, #400
Walnut Creek, CA 94596
http://www.LCoastPress.com

ISBN 978-1-59874-592-4 hardcover
ISBN 978-1-59874-593-1 paperback

Library of Congress Cataloging-in-Publication Data:
Leavy, Patricia, 1975- Essentials of transdisciplinary research : using problem-centered methodologies / Patricia Leavy.
    p. cm.—(Qualitative essentials)
 Includes bibliographical references and index.
 ISBN 978-1-59874-592-4 (hbk. : alk. paper)—ISBN 978-1-59874-593-1 (pbk. : alk. paper)
 1. Social sciences—Research—Methodology. 2. Interdisciplinary research—Methodology. 3. Qualitative research—Methodology. I. Title.
 H61.L4194 2011
 001.4'2—dc23
                        201102231

Printed in the United States of America

⊗™ The paper used in this publication meets the minimum requirements of American National Standard for Information Sciences—Permanence of Paper for Printed Library Materials, ANSI/NISO Z39.48–1992.

CONTENTS

To all of my students, past and present,
and two in particular,
Meaghan Stiman and Lauren Sardi

Preface

If you are possessed by an idea, you find it expressed everywhere, you even smell it.

—Thomas Mann

I recently took my daughter to see the movie "The Last Airbender." She loved the book series and was desperate to see the movie. I had no expectations of enjoying anything other than her company and a bucket of salty popcorn. To my surprise, I was utterly enthralled from the start. The story is set in a fantasy world with four warring groups, each harnessing the power of one of the natural elements. The four groups are: the Fire Nation, the Water Tribe, the Air Nomads, and the Earth Kingdom. Greed, division, and the quest for total power (and arguably fear) caused the Fire Nation to pursue domination at any cost. The Fire Nation murdered all of the Air Nomads because they learned the next Avatar would come from that group. The Avatar is a being with the power to use all four elements and thus prevent the domination of one group over another. Despite the brutal attack of the Fire Nation one Air Nomad remained, quite literally, frozen in time. He is the last living air bender and he is The Avatar. In this epic morality tale, balance between the elements is needed in order to bring peace. The only hope for restoring balance lives within the one who can harness the collective power of all the great elements: The Avatar.

When the movie ended my daughter, practically bouncing in her seat, said, "I loved it! Did you like it, Mom?"

I replied, "I loved it, too! It reminded me of the book I am writing. I couldn't stop thinking about it. The story was a perfect metaphor for my book."

The story of "The Last Airbender" is in many ways the story of the academic research community. We all entered the academy wanting to do good, important work. We wanted to make a difference, discover the unknown, and find solutions to problems that matter. However, academic life can grow the gap between our ideals and our reality. The structure of academia shuffles the social sciences into one building, the natural sciences into another, the computer sciences into yet another, the humanities into yet another, and so on. Further divisions occur as sociologists, psychologists, anthropologists and political scientists are separated, and so, too, with the other fields of inquiry. Then there are divisions within disciplines as a result of competing paradigms and the like. Faced with ticking tenure clocks and the mantra of "publish or perish," researchers (even if unintentionally) reinforce disciplinary boundaries with the projects they take on, the approaches to research they employ, and the venues in which they publish. In this context it is easy to become very busy while in actuality accomplishing very little with respect to the "big picture." It is also easy to become accustomed to justifying the disciplinary borders that we continually re-create—to stake out authoritative claim over domains of inquiry in order to feel relevant. In short, it is not hard to see how the Fire Nation came to think they could function alone and as a result became so disconnected and so arrogant.

The message in "The Last Airbender" is clear: communities with different strengths and capabilities need to work together harmoniously, synergistically. All of the natural elements—fire, water, earth and air—are necessary in a balanced world. They can be put into the service of humanity only if used in complementary ways and not put in opposition to each other. The same is true for the research community and our respective disciplines. Humanity is facing a host of very real and pressing problems—such as violence, sustainability, and health and well-being—and these problems do not exist discreetly in the domain of only one disciplinary purview. Rather, if the research community is to seriously engage with the major issues and problems of our time, we need to pool our resources in the service of addressing complex contemporary problems. Transdisciplinarity provides a pathway.

What Is Transdisciplinarity?

Transdisciplinarity is an approach to conducting social research that involves synergistic collaboration between two or more disciplines with high levels of integration between the disciplinary sets of knowledge. Transdisciplinary research practices are issue- or problem-centered and prioritize the problem at the center of research over discipline-specific concerns, theories or methods. Transdisciplinary research is responsive to (public) needs. Methodologically, transdisciplinary research follows responsive or iterative methodologies and requires innovation, creativity, and flexibility and often employs participatory research design strategies. Transdisciplinarity has the potential to greatly enhance public scholarship.

The Goals of This Book

I have three main goals in writing this book. First, I aim to identify the shift towards transdisciplinarity that is occurring within the research community. Many researchers across the disciplines have been doing transdisciplinary research for decades, although they do not always label it as such. Moreover, both undergraduate and graduate students are increasingly expected to be able to think analytically, critically, conceptually and in integrated ways in order to be effective citizens and laborers in the contemporary world. Therefore, it is important to bring together and name the transdisciplinary efforts underway. Second, I aim to make a case for the importance of promoting transdisciplinary approaches to research. There is a social justice or moral underpinning to transdisciplinary research, as I hope will be evidenced throughout this book. Therefore, I intend to make a case for the importance and usefulness of transdisciplinary approaches to research. This is not to imply that transdisciplinarity is the solution to all of our contemporary problems, nor is it the appropriate approach for all research projects. However, I believe it is clear that transdisciplinary approaches to research are needed in order to effectively address many contemporary challenges. Finally, I hope to provide an introductory guide through research design in order to assist students and researchers trying to build transdisciplinary research projects. While over the past two decades there have been several important books that have addressed shifts towards transdisciplinary research, far less has been done with respect to modeling research design strategies.

In this regard I suggest how researchers might design transdisciplinary projects, and I offer examples of some of the major methodological genres in which transdisciplinarity is flourishing.

The Organization of the Book

In chapter 1 I provide a consolidated review of four modes of knowledge production: disciplinary, multi-disciplinary, interdisciplinary, and transdisciplinary. I also discuss the relationship between disciplinary training and transdisciplinary approaches to research.

In chapter 2 I situate the emergence of transdisciplinary research practices in a larger context, noting important shifts both within academia and beyond academia. Towards this end I review the impact of the social justice movements on research practice, including the development of critical theories and critical area studies. I also discuss how changes with respect to globalization and technology have impacted research practice.

Chapter 3 focuses on the major transdisciplinary research design features. The chapter covers the research design features necessary to develop an issue- or problem-centered methodological strategy. In this regard I review research design, data collection, analysis and interpretation, representation and dissemination. The chapter also offers suggestions for how to build a transdisciplinary research project as a sole researcher, a member of a multi-disciplinary research team, or as a member of a research partnership involving non-academic stakeholders.

Chapter 4 reviews transdisciplinary approaches to community-based research and chapter 5 reviews transdisciplinary approaches to arts-based research. Both chapters cover the major tenets of these research genres, the advantages of working within the genres, major research design features, and the potential for public policy development. In the chapter on community-based research I also review transnational research partnerships. In the chapter on arts-based research I focus on performance-based approaches to research as a means of engaging the public.

Finally, chapter 6 reviews the primary principles upon which transdisciplinary research might be evaluated. Moreover, I provide a review of strategies for enhancing the credibility of transdisciplinary research findings. The chapter concludes with a discussion of how to move the research community forward. In this regard I analyze the organization of academic life and in particular tenure and promotion structures, publishing issues and funding.

It is important to note that there are clear limitations to this book. There are many challenges when writing a book about an emerging and highly diffuse body of work. No one book can cover it all. Therefore I have had to make many choices which some will agree with or disagree with to varying degrees. For example, it would take a whole book to properly cover the continuum of disciplinarity to multi-disciplinarity to interdisciplinarity to transdisciplinarity. I had to make decisions about which thinkers and theories to include, and I realize that for every inclusion there are more omissions. However, as a primary goal was to provide a model for research design, which is what I believe is most lacking in the current literature, I had to consolidate the discussion of these other important issues. In this regard I also had to make choices about which research genres to include. Some will no doubt disagree with my choice to include arts-based research over other possibilities, for example. I understand this. As I am of course positioned within this work I included those genres I am most connected with. However, as I note repeatedly, the methods, strategies, and research genres I review are meant only as examples which I hope will prompt readers to think about related issues when working within other research genres. Remember, "Ideas won't keep: something must be done about them" (Alfred North Whitehead). I hope this book is one step towards that end.

Acknowledgments

I am very grateful to the many people who supported the writing of this book. First and foremost, a spirited thank you to Mitch Allen, publisher extraordinaire. Your unique vision for the field and willingness to innovate allowed this book to happen. Thank you! Likewise, a hearty thanks to Jan Morse. I greatly value your support and guidance. My gratitude to the entire Left Coast team, particularly Michael Jennings for his extensive copy editing and Hannah Jennings for her design work, as well as the reviewers whose feedback helped me refine my thinking. Next, my sincere thanks to all those whose work I refer to in this book. You are all the true pioneers and my teachers. I wish to thank Stonehill College for supporting this work through a summer grant. In this regard a special thanks to Provost Katie Conboy and Dean Joe Favazza. My sincere appreciation to

Betsy Dean for her outstanding work preparing the index. Thank you, Betsy, for providing this service to Stonehill faculty. Thank you to my outstanding research assistant Shalen Lowell, without whom this book would surely be one big mess. A very special thank you to my family for the love and laughter. I am deeply grateful to my incredible husband, Mark Robins, for his unfailing support, and my daughter Madeline, for her unrelenting optimism. Love you both more than all the words. Finally, I dedicate this book to all of my students who are amongst my greatest teachers. In particular, thank you to Meaghan Stiman and Lauren Sardi for your research assistance, support, inspiration and friendship. You are the future of the research community!

Chapter One

Transdisciplinarity
Disciplinary to Transdisciplinary Knowledge-Building

Disciplines, like nations, are a necessary evil that enable human beings of bounded rationality to simplify the structure of their goals. But parochialism is everywhere, and the world sorely needs international and interdisciplinary travelers who will carry new knowledge from one enclave to another.

—Nobel Prize recipient, Herbert Simon (1992, 269)

The international research community has entered a new era characterized by *transdisciplinary research practices*. The cumulative impact of transdisciplinary perspectives and innovations is a new paradigm. Over the last few decades transdisciplinarity has grown rapidly in medical/ health research, environmental research, sustainability research, educational research, policy research, and social research. The main focus of this book is on transdisciplinarity in relation to social research questions that often originate in the social sciences, education and health studies.

As will be noted throughout this book, the beginnings of scholarship were actually more transdisciplinary than we have seen over the past century. From early links between mathematics and poetry, astronomy and mythology, and science and rhetoric, holistic approaches to knowledge-building developed as a result of an emphasis on idea generation. The disciplining of knowledge-building practices was constructed as a means of organizing universities far more than advancing ideas. Interestingly, despite the disciplining of research institutions, which in turn require undergraduate and graduate students to specialize in at least one discipline, most universities and colleges require students to take core courses that often focus on the early holistic "thinkers" such as early Greek or Renaissance scholarship—I myself was required to take several such courses. With this said, the modern academy has been based on the creation and maintenance of disciplinary borders. Therefore, the recent growth in transdisciplinary approaches to research signifies a major turn in how social research is conceived and conducted. The deep sharing of information and research tools across disciplinary borders and the development of new conceptual frameworks have been important and fruitful with respect to moving the scientific community forward in three major ways.

First, it has freed researchers from the limits of working with their disciplinary tools alone. This has fostered an enormous expansion of social research. Second, the ability to use additional tools and resources has allowed research questions to be asked from more diverse perspectives. Increased empirical diversity has also facilitated theoretical advancements as well as the realization of theoretical promises. Third, and perhaps most significantly, the transdisciplinarity of research methods has caused an erosion of the basis upon which disciplinary borders have historically been formed and maintained. This has prompted a series of re-evaluations of research tools as well as scientific criteria for evaluating research. Concurrently, as borders shift, new research collaborations have led to the asking of new research questions and the creation of new, hybrid research tools, designed to address those questions. These factors have culminated in the development of transdisciplinary research practices.

Transdisciplinarity is an approach to conducting social research. Transdisciplinary research practices are issue- or problem-centered approaches to research that prioritize the problem at the center of research over discipline-specific concerns, theories or methods. Transdisciplinary research is responsive to (public) needs. Transdisciplinary research practices transcend disciplinary borders and open up entirely new research pathways. Transdisciplinarity produces new knowledge-building practices.

Furthermore, transdisciplinary practices are forging coalitions and collaborations across disciplinary and geographic borders. The merging of different national perspectives, coupled with cross-disciplinary pollination, is vital towards making academic research an authentic part of the globalized world it claims to study. In this regard, transdisciplinary practices have forged a growing transnational research community. Moreover, transdisciplinary approaches to research are extending public scholarship and promoting research practices that engage with public needs.

All disciplines offer unique but limited perspectives onto the social reality they study. By cultivating these perspectives in academic training and then liberating researchers from working exclusively within their confines, the research community is able to go further than ever before in our quest to understand and intervene in our rapidly changing world. The implications are both theoretical and methodological. It is an exciting time.

The Continuum: Disciplinarity, Multi-Disciplinarity, Interdisciplinarity and Transdisciplinarity

Before reviewing the major approaches to research, and the extent to which each prompts interaction (and in some cases integration) among disciplines (Flinterman, Teclemariam-Mesbach, Broerse & Bunders 2001), it is important to note that there is nothing inherently good or bad about any of these approaches. Different research topics, purposes and questions may lead to different approaches. In some contexts a disciplinary approach may be what is required, whereas in others a transdisciplinary approach may yield more fruitful results. It is important, however, that as a research community we embrace these different approaches so that we expand the possible topics and questions we can address, not limit them. The goal of this book is to review transdisciplinary approaches and therefore I compare disciplinary, multi, inter, and transdisciplinary approaches—placing them on a continuum and pointing to their differences and limitations. In this chapter I will use the example of "bullying" in order to show how disciplinary, multi-disciplinary, interdisciplinary and transdisciplinary approaches may lead researchers to tackle this topic differently. I have selected the topic of bullying because it is of wide-reaching concern to researchers across the social and behavioral sciences, education and the humanities. While I ultimately focus on the strengths and *usefulness* of transdisciplinarity, this is in no way meant to minimize the important research conducted from these other approaches. Moreover, when speaking in generalizations (which out of necessity I do when reviewing the characteristics of each approach), there will of course be claims made that do not fit every research project. As Lincoln and Guba famously observed, "The trouble with generalizations is that they don't apply to particulars" (2000, 27).

Disciplinarity

Historically, knowledge has been produced within disciplines (or mono-disciplines as they are sometimes called). Disciplines remain the most common sites for knowledge generation. When thinking about how disciplines function, the term "disciplinary codes" (Steinmetz 2007) is useful because it implies that disciplines have ritualized or coded ways of building, evaluating and disseminating knowledge.

In the simplest of terms disciplines are detailed knowledge areas with distinct borders. Disciplines have common research objects, questions, methodological tools and exemplary cases (Greckhamer, Koro-Ljung-berg, Sebnem & Hayes 2008). Here are a couple of examples of how researchers applying a disciplinary lens might come to study bullying:

- ➤ A Psychologist may develop a small-scale research project in order to examine the psychological effects of bullying on the bullied in a particular environment. Theories and methods commonly used in psychology, such as cognitive interviewing, would be employed.

- ➤ A Sociologist may develop a small-scale research project in order to examine the role of peer culture in bullying (such as the social structure of popularity within a school context). Theories and methods commonly used in sociology, such as ethnography or questionnaires, would be employed.

Disciplines also have prevailing worldviews or paradigms that are widely shared (Greckhamer et al. 2008; Kuhn 1996). This is evidenced in the preceding examples. The psychologist is applying a psychological perspective as he or she considers the issue of bullying and therefore is guided by a focus on psychological processes and/or outcomes. In contrast, the sociologist is guided by a sociological perspective as he or she considers the issue of bullying and therefore is guided by a focus on the social context in which bullying occurs.

Of course some disciplines are characterized by further divisions where multiple and competing paradigms co-exist and, at times, challenge and push each other (such as the qualitative and quantitative paradigms in sociology and psychology, for example). Nevertheless, each discipline has one or more shared sets of assumptions about how research ought to be conducted. The assumptions are not "natural" but rather constructed by those within the discipline. Disciplines are created and sustained by the definitions members of the discipline create and maintain (P. Berger, B. Berger & Keller 1973). It is in this way that "disciplinary codes" and disciplinary lenses become normalized.

Professionals within disciplines also develop a shared language or "disciplinary discourse" (Greckhamer et al. 2008; Klein 1990). Disciplinarity breeds isolation and exclusivity with respect to other disciplines because, in part, it is difficult to communicate without a shared language (Austin, Park & Goble 2008). Disciplines do much more, however, than tell researchers what to study and how to study it. They in fact become communities in which researchers operate. Each community has its own set of professional expectations and demands. In short, pressures. Disciplines serve to create the kinds of researchers we become by organizing research activities and professional development, thus building professional identities. For example, disciplines dictate what professional activities are appropriate and what knowledge will be recognized and valued (including what will be published, what will receive funding, what will earn faculty tenure). Therefore, embedded within the context of institutionalized incentives, disciplinary structures determine what knowledge will be produced (Greckhamer et al. 2008). As Greckhamer and colleagues observe, disciplines "control and standardize knowledge production" (p. 312). Kuhn (1963) famously noted that members of disciplines are specialists who together build a scientific community based on shared assumptions. Kuhn further explained, "Members communicate with their community, share basic assumptions and examples about meaningful problems, standards, for reliable and valid methods, as well as what is considered a good solution to a problem" (quoted by Hadorn, Hoffmann-Riem, Biber-Klemm, Grossenbacker-Mansuy, Joye, Pohl, Weismann & Zemp 2008, 27–28). The stronger disciplinary boundaries have become, the more pressure there has been for further specialization even within one's own discipline. As a result, the range of what one can study has become more narrowly defined. As specialization has increased, researchers have followed the same career paths, and thus disciplinarity has become further institutionalized. So the question becomes: is there another path?

> Two roads diverged in a wood, and I—
> I took the one less traveled by
> And that has made all the difference.
>
> (Robert Frost, The Road Not Taken, 1920)

Many scholars suggest that research approaches in which different disciplines interact and/or integrate (such as interdisciplinary and transdisciplinary approaches) expose the limitations of disciplinarity (for example see Klein 2004). Narrow experts cannot address the fundamental issues facing humanity in contemporary society (Klein 2004). As interdisciplinary and transdisciplinary scholars suggest, social problems and issues don't develop according to our disciplinary structure. Mittelstrass (1992) expresses this well: "Nowadays, problems seldom do us the favor of letting themselves be defined according to the order of our scientific habits" (as quoted in Pohl & Hadorn 2007). Many problems are by nature transdisciplinary and, therefore, so must be our attempts to deal with them. As suggested earlier, this does not necessarily mean we abandon our disciplinary training.

Multi-Disciplinarity and Interdisciplinarity

Multi-, inter, (and trans) disciplinarity, in that order, exist on a continuum of increasing interaction and integration between disciplines. Newell (2000) provides the following model for thinking about the continuum of interaction between disciplines, beginning with the least level of disciplinary interaction (multi-disciplinary):

- *cooperate* (disciplines engage in parallel play);
- *appreciate* (disciplines come to understand each other's perspective);
- *dismantle* (disciplines bring to light and debate each other's assumptions);
- *reconstruct* (disciplines work together to develop overarching concepts);
- *modify* (disciplines shift time-horizon assumptions, or methods to collaborate); and
- *transform* (disciplines are so altered that they cannot return to business as usual). (p. 230)

Multi-Disciplinarity

Multi-disciplinary approaches to research involve collaboration between two or more disciplines on a research project; however, each discipline maintains its own assumptions, values, and methods. In other words, each discipline maintains its autonomy during the collaboration (Wickson,

Carew & Russell 2006). Borders are left intact during multi-disciplinary collaboration as distinct disciplines "co-exist" within a project (Johnson 2001, 270). Returning to the bullying example we can see this at work:

→ A Psychologist and a Sociologist may partner to conduct research on bullying in schools. Each researcher would separately create his or her agenda and research protocol, with minimal, if any, collaboration. For example, the Psychologist might engage in a cognitive interviewing protocol in order to develop a profile of the effect of bullying on the bullied. The Sociologist might conduct in-depth interviews with school age children in order to understand the peer culture in which bullying occurs. The researchers may co-author an article in which they each review their findings, or separately author discipline-specific articles.

Austin and colleagues (2008) define multi-disciplinary approaches as, "representatives from several disciplines, each contributing particular knowledge and methods from their respective fields" (p. 557). Similarly, Russell, Wickson and Carew (2008) write: "Disciplinary specialists work together maintaining their disciplinary approaches and perspectives" (p. 460). Other definitions of multidisciplinarity point to the inherent limitations of these approaches. For example, Flinterman and colleagues (2001) offer the following definition: "When a variety of disciplines collaborate in one research program without integration of concepts, epistemologies, or methodologies... the degree of integration between disciplines is restricted to the linking of research results" (p. 257). The word "linking" is important as it connotes a scenario in which research results are "added" to each other, in which one set of results "augments" another. In this respect McDonell (2000) notes that researchers have an "associative" relationship in multi-disciplinary projects and each "adds" their work to the others' (p. 27). Many scholars note a major limitation of multi-disciplinary research is the lack of "cross-fertilization" between disciplines because the disciplines remain "self contained," and therefore there is a lack of "synergy" among outcomes (for example see Bruce, Lyall, Tait & Williams 2004; Hadorn et al. 2008). (As will be noted shortly, *synergy* is a key factor that distinguishes transdisciplinarity from all other models of knowledge production.) Given the lack of synergy present in multi-disciplinary collaborations, it is not surprising that some scholars suggest the outcome of the research may not be greater than the sum of its parts (McMichael 2000).

There is also the issue of the kinds of research topics that are likely to prompt multi-disciplinary partnerships. Because disciplinary methodologies are maintained, multi-disciplinary research projects usually involve researching disciplinary themes or topics (Wickson et al. 2006) and thus do not necessarily inspire the asking of radically different research questions. In this respect, multi-disciplinary approaches to research essentially offer a slightly broader perspective or multi-perspectival view on traditional research questions.

Interdisciplinarity

Interdisciplinary approaches to research also involve collaborations between researchers from two or more disciplines. It is generally understood that there is a greater level of interaction between the disciplines in interdisciplinary research. However, it is not surprising that the literature on interdisciplinarity presents a wide array of views on how interdisciplinarity works and how much interaction and integration is actually fostered in these partnerships. While there are many nuances I am not going to address, for simplicity I suggest that the two major lines of thought center on whether or not disciplines maintain clear distinctions in interdisciplinary work.

Some researchers contend that, as with multi-disciplinary research, disciplinary borders are maintained in interdisciplinary research (Steinmetz 2007). In this vein, some view interdisciplinarity as a "process of juxtapositioning" disciplines (Cameron & Mengler 2009, 194), which implies the disciplines involved still maintain their autonomy. Masini (2000) refers to interdisciplinarity as a "parallel analysis" of the issue under investigation (p. 120).

Other researchers suggest that differing from multi-disciplinary research, interdisciplinary approaches to research may call into question the assumptions of the disciplines involved in the project; therefore, new assumptions may emerge as a result of the collaboration (Austin et al. 2008). In this respect, Austin and colleagues view the core of interdisciplinary research as *emergence*—"emergence," they write, "of new concepts, problems, or solutions being supported by a synthesis of diverse perspectives" (2008, 560). Similarly, Flinterman and colleagues note that "concepts, methodologies, or epistemologies are explicitly exchanged and integrated, resulting in a mutual enrichment" (2001, 257). Differing from his contention that multi-disciplinary research represents an "associative" relationship among the disciplines involved, McDonell

(2000) suggests that in interdisciplinary research the relationship is "relational" and the collaboration involves each discipline taking on some of the assumptions of the others (p. 27). Further, interdisciplinary work involves the creation of "a shared methodological approach" which crosses disciplinary boundaries (Wickson et al. 2006, 1050). However, even researchers who suggest that interdisciplinarity promotes exchange and emergence may still concede that disciplines and their guiding approaches are left intact, even if combined. For example, Wickson and colleagues note that interdisciplinarity "involves developing a common framework within which distinct epistemological approaches are used to investigate different themes or aspects of a research problem" (2006, 1050). Within this framework methods may be transferred from one discipline to another (Pohl et al. 2007). Returning to our bullying example we can see this at play:

→ The Psychologist and Sociologist may come together in order to brainstorm about their approach to the topic. Upon learning of the relevant theories and methods of the other discipline, the two may develop a shared framework, such as a psychosocial approach to bullying. Such an approach may consider the psychological profile of the bullied in relation to a range of factors within their peer culture as well as the dynamics between the bullied, bully and peers (bystanders) within the school environment. Applying this framework, the researchers may build a mixed-methods design (perhaps using questionnaires and interviews), collect the data and engage in a shared analysis and interpretation process resulting in a co-authored article or series of co-authored or individually authored articles. (This would be the "best" or most integrative version of interdisciplinarity.)

Not only are there different philosophical perspectives on interdisciplinarity—the promise and perils—there is also clearly a range of applications of interdisciplinarity. In other words, there is a continuum on which interdisciplinary research can be placed with respect to key issues such as interaction, integration, synergy and emergence.

Space constraints do not allow for an in-depth discussion of this issue; however, I would like to put forth some suggested criteria for evaluating the intensity of interdisciplinarity in a project which may be useful when judging the extent to which various research projects engage with the possibilities of interdisciplinarity. First, I again suggest that the appropriateness of "degrees of interdisciplinarity," if you will, should be based on the particulars of any given research project; there is no one way to be interdisciplinary.

Flinterman and colleagues suggest that "degrees of interdisciplinarity" result from the "degree of exchange and integration and the differences in the paradigms between the disciplines involved" (2001, 257). The issues of exchange and integration are sometimes difficult to evaluate but will be reviewed throughout this book. The distance between paradigms, however, is much clearer. For example, a project concerning several disciplines operating from a positivist point of view may not be considered highly interdisciplinary because the values, assumptions and methodologies guiding the research process are reinforced by each discipline, not challenged and changed. This may be a perfectly appropriate arrangement for a particular project—the point is not to rank the merit of various collaborations, but simply to note the differences among these kinds of collaborations and the "level" of interdisciplinarity. By these criteria the bullying example in which both researchers came from the social sciences and developed a shared but ultimately social scientific framework may not be considered highly interdisciplinary.

Nissani (1995) suggests that the four criteria for understanding the level of interdisciplinarity in a project should be: 1) the number of disciplines involved, 2) the distance between the disciplines involved, 3) the novelty and creativity in combining disciplinary elements, and 4) the degree of integration.

Now of course when put into practice this is all very complex. For example, a project may have a great number of highly diverse disciplines participating, but there may be little integration; therefore, the project may in fact meet the requirements of traditional multi-disciplinary research far more than interdisciplinary. Likewise, in such a project, some disciplines may have their values, assumptions, and methodologies more highly valued by the research partners than some others. In this instance there may be very little creativity or integration. Moreover, what does it mean to claim various disciplines are involved in a project if one world view (or paradigm) dominates the project? There is an issue of power that permeates all research collaborations: the power of individuals involved to shape and guide the process and/or outcomes as well as the power of disciplines and their dominant paradigms to dominate the process and/or outcomes (Austin et al. 2008). This is just one example of how complicated "evaluating" interdisciplinarity is when applied to actual research contexts. I should also note that many proponents of transdisciplinary approaches to research suggest that the fourth criterion, integration, has not been realized in interdisciplinary efforts and it is only at the point of integration that transdisciplinarity emerges (see Austin et al. 2008). Nevertheless, Nissani provides a useful framework for thinking about the issues on which research claiming to be interdisciplinary can vary greatly. It is not surprising that, as reviewed, philosophical perspectives on what constitutes interdisciplinarity, and how it differs from multi-disciplinarity, vary widely.

With respect to research topics and questions, topics that are likely to be investigated are not discipline-based like in multi-disciplinary research but rather "occupy space between existing disciplines" (McMichael 2000, 203). Russell and colleagues suggest that interdisciplinary research generally focuses on "areas of overlap or intersection between disciplines" (2008, 460). As many topical areas are of interest to researchers in multiple disciplines (for example, bullying is of interest to sociologists, psychologists, social workers, and education researchers), similarly to multi-disciplinarity, interdisciplinary collaborations may involve the asking of essentially traditional research questions but from more than one perspective.

Before moving into a discussion of transdisciplinarity, the heart of this undertaking, it is important to mention that the relationship between interdisciplinarity and disciplinarity is a contested area in the literature, and one that I believe has lead to the emergence of a rapidly growing community of proponents of transdisciplinarity. Many on the frontlines of transdisciplinary approaches to research suggest that even interdisciplinary collaborations presuppose disciplines and therefore do not challenge the disciplinary organization of knowledge (Abbott 2001; Greckhamer et al. 2008). Some go further to suggest that interdisciplinarity actually serves to "further strengthen and reproduce disciplinarity" (Greckhamer et al. 2008, 324). Derrida (1997) suggests that interdisciplinarity actually confirms disciplinarity (despite the fears initially surrounding moves towards interdisciplinarity in academia). Drawing on Derrida (1997), Greckhamer and colleagues (2008) explain that interdisciplinarity is enabled through the existence of disciplines; therefore, that which makes interdisciplinarity possible also makes it, in its pure form, impossible. For some, transdisciplinarity represents a way to overcome this paradox and *transcend* disciplinarity.

Transdisciplinarity

It is important to acknowledge that multi-disciplinarity and interdisciplinarity have contributed enormously to moving the research community forward by getting disciplines to think about how they are related to each other and to start working together on issues of import. Moreover, these two approaches to research have implicitly exposed the limitations of disciplinarity. Nevertheless, these approaches can only go and have only gone so far. Some researchers argue that multi-disciplinary and interdisciplinary approaches to research have an additive quality (Ismail 2000) and fail to integrate and synthesize disciplinary knowledges. Transdisciplinarity has emerged in order to meet the promise of transcending disciplinary knowledge production in order to more effectively address real-world issues and problems. In this vein many suggest that interdisciplinarity turns into transdisciplinarity in a given project via transcendence and deep levels of collaboration (see for example Austin et al. 2008; Depres, Brais & Avellan 2004; Flinterman et al. 2001; Giri 2002; Klein 2004; Ramadier 2004) or via a participatory approach (ProClim 1997).

The origins of the term "transdisciplinary" can be traced to the early 1970s and the first international conference on interdisciplinarity (Klein et al. 2001). Jean Piaget and Erich Jantsch each pioneered the theoretical conceptualization of transdisciplinarity. The concept of transdisciplinarity is attributed to Piaget, who believed that "the maturation of general structures and fundamental patterns of thought across fields would lead to a general theory of systems or structures" (Klein 2004, 515). Jantsch is also credited as one of the first proponents of transdisciplinarity. He defined transdisciplinarity as "the co-ordination of all disciplines and interdisciplines in the education innovation system on the basis of a generalized axiomatics (introduced from the purposive level down) and an emerging epistemological ('synepistemic') pattern" (Jantsch 1972, 106). Put more simply, Jantsch saw transdisciplinarity as a means of addressing a social or human purpose, and he "envisioned a multi-level systematic coordination of research, innovation, and education" (Klein 2004, 515). Although definitions of the term vary enormously, following Piaget and Jantsch transdisciplinarity is generally understood as an approach to research that involves the integration of multiple disciplines in a project aimed at a social, human or "life-world" purpose.[1] It is also clear that transdisciplinarity grew out of interdisciplinarity or is a particular thread of interdisciplinarity (which will be discussed in chapter 2) (see for example Austin et al. 2008; Depres et al. 2004; Flinterman et al. 2001; Giri 2002; Klein 2004; Ramadier 2004).

In essence, transdisciplinarity presupposes that contemporary social/human issues and problems can only be understood and solved if viewed holistically and not artificially broken down into narrow research purposes that suit different disciplinary lenses. Herbert Simon, 1978 Nobel Prize recipient in Economic Science, expresses this well.

> To understand budget decisions, one has to understand decision making in general.... It is necessary to study... the process of human thinking. To study thinking, I had to abandon my home discipline of political science and economics... for the alien shores of psychology, and a little later, of computer science and artificial intelligence." (1992, 265)

Many researchers suggest that transdisciplinarity is not a method for doing research or an outcome of research but rather an *approach* to the research process (Lawrence & Depres 2004; Klein 2004) or a "new way of thinking" (Giri 2002, 103). In this regard, Mittelstrass asserts that even though theoretical work may emerge from transdisciplinary research, transdisciplinarity is a "research principle" first and foremost (1996, 329). There is much debate in the literature about what the term transdisciplinary means and what constitutes transdisciplinary research. Although I will present various definitions of the term prior to presenting my own broad view I should note from the outset that I find any sort of definition problematic for three primary reasons.

First, definitions always represent a form of closure, and I think researchers should be free to label their work as they see fit; those who read their work can of course judge it as they see fit and determine how useful it is or isn't to them.

Second, the literature explicitly on transdisciplinarity has emerged disproportionately in a few fields and on a few topics (medicine, environmental studies/sustainability), and therefore there are inherent biases (points of view) that are more strongly represented than others. In this book I adopt the point of view of a researcher coming from the social sciences.

Third, the literature on transdisciplinarity is relatively new and thus, as an emerging field, there is a flurry of ongoing debate and negotiation taking place. Sometimes this kind of debate prompts folks to take very strong positions, to set forth rigid frameworks that may work for their current research but that do not necessarily work for everyone and in every context.

All of this is an important part of moving the discussion forward, but in the interest of making this book useful to those in the social sciences, education and health studies who may be interested in engaging with transdisciplinarity, I think it is best to focus on some of the principles of transdisciplinarity without putting forth a definition that may be limiting. The fear associated with this is of course that people may think "anything goes"; however, as will be reviewed throughout this book regardless of what we call our research (i.e., "transdisciplinary") we are still obliged to create a methodologically sound research project (strategies for research design and evaluation are given in-depth treatment in chapters 3 through 6). With all of this said, I begin reviewing some definitions of transdisciplinarity as well as the main principles of transdisciplinarity that emerge consistently in the literature. Finally, in consideration of the "agreed upon" principles I present my own broad view of transdisciplinary research.

Definitions of Transdisciplinarity

Perspectives on transdisciplinarity vary greatly in the literature, and there is little consensus regarding how to define the term (as would be expected with an emergent and inherently diffuse approach to research).

Some scholars explain that beyond multiple disciplinary bodies coming together, researchers should partner with practitioners or other stakeholders outside of academia in their research in order to address "real-world" problems (for example see Burger & Kamber 2003; Haberli & Grossenbacher-Mansuy 1998; Klein 2001). In this regard, transdisciplinarity can be understood as an attempt to bridge the academic world and the needs of different social bodies to address real-world issues and problems (Hadorn et al. 2008; Hoffman-Riem, Biber-Klemm, Grossenbacher-Mansuy, Hadorn, Joye, Pohl, Wiesmann & Zemp 2008).

Some scholars provide general definitions of transdisciplinarity that call out the general character of such approaches. For example, Krimsky explains transdisciplinarity as "the transcendence of disciplines for addressing meta-questions; the intersection of two or more disciplines for explicating problems; and the combination of methods/techniques/theory for several disciplines in the framing or testing of a hypothesis" (2000, 111). Of course researchers can adapt these ideas to fit with their research project. For instance, instead of posing or testing a hypothesis (more often done in quantitative research), a researcher or team of researchers may be framing a research purpose with related research questions (more often done in qualitative research).

Many researchers suggest specific criteria that denote transdisciplinarity. Pohl and Hadorn provide a definition which is representative of many of the models that appear in the literature. They assert transdisciplinary research

> deals with problem fields in such a way that it can: a) grasp the complexity of problems, b) take into account the diversity of life-world and scientific perceptions of problems, c) link abstract and case-specific knowledge, and d) develop knowledge and practices that promote what is perceived to be the common good. (2008, 20)

Summing up the literature on transdisciplinarity, Hadorn and colleagues set forth a similar set of four criteria: "first the focus on life-world problems; second the transcending and integrating of disciplinary paradigms; third participatory research; and fourth the search for unity of knowledge beyond disciplines" (2008, 29). Hadorn and colleagues go on to explain, and I concur, that the first two criteria are widely agreed upon, with increasing debate and disagreement with respect to the third and fourth criteria.

As opposed to formulating a set of particular criteria, some scholars explain the tenets of transdisciplinarity in more general terms. For example, Klein characterizes transdisciplinarity as a "mode of thought and action" (2004, 24). She explains transdisciplinarity as "a process and a commitment to a way of knowing and a way of being" (2000, 216). Klein provides the following definition: "Transdisciplinary vision, which replaces reduction with a new principle of relativity, is transcultural, transnational, and encompasses ethics, spirituality, and creativity" (2004, 516).

Klein further suggests that transdisciplinarity is a fluid concept that can be defined as "a holistic vision; a particular method, concept or theory; a general attitude of openness and a capacity for collaboration; as well as an essential strategy for solving complex problems" (2000, 4).

Similarly to Klein's position that transdisciplinarity is a vision, Leroy has suggested transdisciplinarity is a "sensitizing concept" (Klein 2004). Other scholars talk about transdisciplinarity as "a field of relationships" (Giri 2002, 106). This is because a transdisciplinary orientation requires researchers to look at disciplines in relational terms, not oppositional terms, which may require exploring possible pathways of interaction and then creating those relationships among disciplines (Giri 2002).

Other researchers elucidate the tenets of transdisciplinarity by explaining the ways in which it moves beyond interdisciplinarity. For example, Austin and colleagues write:

> Transdisciplinary research occurs when the collaborative process is taken one step further, often spontaneously emerging from interdisciplinary research when discipline-transcending concepts, terminology, and methods evolve to create a higher level framework and a fundamental epistemological shift occurs (Giri 2002; Max-Neef 2005). This step requires mutual interpretation of disciplinary knowledge (Gibbons et al. 1994) and a coherent reconfiguration of the situation. (2008, 557)

Other researchers explain the inter-trans relationship differently. Depres and colleagues assert that even in transdisciplinary projects the research group (or I would suggest, the research resources, which may or may not involve experts from different disciplines) "always remain interdisciplinary by the very nature of disciplinary education, and the research itself, which, if transdisciplinary, implies the final knowledge is more than the sum of its disciplinary components" (Lawrence & Depres 2004, 400).

With respect to the example of bullying, a transdisciplinary approach is problem-centered, and thus disciplinary resources are brought in based on their relevance and deep collaboration is demanded. For example, the process may look like this:

→ A team of psychologists, sociologists, educational researchers and policy researchers assemble and may partner with non-academic stakeholders such as school teachers, afterschool care program coordinators, PTO members, social workers and guidance counselors.

→ The team spends ample time developing a research agenda: identifying key topics, building shared definitions and concepts, and developing a conceptual framework for the study that is not the property of any one discipline. The team then comes up with a research design aimed at addressing the varied dimensions of the topic, such as: the relationship between the bully, bullied and peer bystanders; the relationship between the bully, bullied and professional bystanders (such as teachers and school workers); the role of public policies in impacting teacher and other professional responses/reactions to bullying; how the structure of the peer culture promotes bullying; the role of cyberculture (such as social networking sites) and other technologies (such as cell phones with cameras) in bullying; how structured leisure time (such as group sports or games) versus independent "free time" impacts bullying; the roles of gender, class, race, ethnicity, religion and sexual orientation in bullying; and so forth.

→ The team then creates a planned division of labor. The research design includes ample time for the team (subsets of the team or the entire team) to come together, share early findings, and renegotiate assumptions and practices.

→ Research findings are presented in multiple and appropriate forms and venues with the goal of reaching different groups of relevant stakeholders in order to promote positive social change.

I now move into a discussion of the principles of transdisciplinarity that permeate the literature.

Principles of Transdisciplinarity

Regardless of particular definitions, transdisciplinarity always involves the collaboration of multiple disciplinary sets of knowledge (I suggest this may be multiple persons working on a project or an individual researcher working with multiple sets of disciplinary knowledge and tools). Transdisciplinarity aims to provide a holistic and synergistic approach to studying an issue or problem. Further, the key principles of transdisciplinarity also include transcendence, emergence, synthesis, integration, innovation and flexibility.

Transdisciplinarity is issue- or problem-generated, not discipline-driven (Krimsky 2000). Traditionally, a researcher's disciplinary training has driven topic selection and question generation. First and foremost, transdisciplinarity is a way of putting the research problem, topic, issue or question at the center of the research process irrespective of one's "home" discipline. The questions for a researcher become transformed from: "What is an acceptable research topic in my discipline, and how does my discipline view this topic?" to: "What issues in the real-world need to be addressed or what problems in the real-world need to be solved, and how can they be most fully addressed? What sets of disciplinary knowledge are useful in this instance, and how will my disciplinary training come to bear?" Transdisciplinarity as an approach has emerged as a way to address important topics and questions, solve real-world problems, and identify and address the needs of an increasingly complex global community.

Table 1.1 Principles of Transdisciplinarity

Principle	Practice
Issue- or Problem-Centered	Problem at center of research determines use of disciplinary resources and guides methodology
Holistic or Synergistic Research Approach	Problem considered holistically through an iterative research process which produces integrated knowledge
Transcendence	Researchers build conceptual frameworks that transcend disciplinary perspectives in order to effectively address the research problem
Emergence	Placing the problem at the center of research (transcending disciplinarity) cultivates the emergence of new conceptual and methodological frameworks
Innovation	Researchers build new conceptual, methodological and theoretical frameworks as needed
Flexibility	Iterative research process requires openness to new ideas and willingness to adapt to new insights

In order to address real-world issues or problems as fully as possible, transdisciplinary approaches to research are *holistic* (see for example Flinterman et al. 2001; Klein 2000; Leavy 2009; Messerli & Messerli 2008). In fact, some suggest that transdisciplinarity is a response to the demand for holistic approaches to knowledge generation (Flinterman et al. 2001). In a transdisciplinary research project the aim is to consider the issue or problem holistically. In this regard, researchers create definitions of key concepts and the like in a holistic manner. The bringing together of different bodies of knowledge, different sets of research tools, and perhaps a team of differently trained researchers (and at times practitioners and/or community members) is intended to occur in a holistic and *integrated* manner. Additionally, a holistic approach to the research process itself is endorsed. This means that all of the aspects of the research methodology are connected and inform each other in an iterative process (Hesse-Biber & Leavy 2011) (explicated later in chapter 3 on research design). Finally, the outcome of this process is an integrated form of knowledge or a hybrid knowledge that is larger than the sum of the parts that went into creating it (Flinterman et al. 2001; Hadorn et al. 2008; Horlick-Jones & Sime 2004; Klein 2004; McDonell 2000; Newell 2000; Pohl et al. 2007). Flinterman and colleagues discuss the relationship between holism and the production of integrated knowledge as follows:

> Transdisciplinarity as a specific form of interdisciplinarity in which boundaries between and beyond disciplines are transcended and knowledge and perspectives from different scientific disciplines as well as nonscientific sources are integrated…. In transdisciplinary research, widely differing forms of knowledge are integrated to produce an overall integral knowledge. (2008, 257)

Related to the idea of a holistic framework and integrated knowledge, many transdisciplinary researchers talk about transdisciplinary approaches to research as *synergistic* (sometimes they write of *synergy*, *synthesis* or *unity of knowledge*) (for example see Hadorn et al. 2008; Klein 2000, 2004; Lawrence 2004; McMichael 2000; Newell 2000; Nicolescu 1996; Pohl et al. 2007).

The term *transcendence* (or *transgression*) consistently appears in the literature on transdisciplinarity (see for example Austin et al. 2008; Bruce et al. 2004; Depres et al. 2004; Lawrence et al. 2004; Flinterman et al. 2001; Giri 2002; Greckhamer et al. 2008; Hadorn et al. 2008; Hoffmann-Riem et al. 2007; Horlick-Jones et al. 2004; Jantsch 1972; Krimsky 2000; McDonell 2000; McMichael 2000; Newell 2000; Nicolescu 1996; Pohl et al. 2007; Russell et al. 2008; Steinmetz 2007). Transdisciplinary approaches to research help researchers to transcend the limitations of disciplinary forms of knowledge-building, organization and dissemination. Because information, data, theories, and methodologies from multiple disciplinary viewpoints are brought into the process, and are respected and combined in order to create something new that is irreducible to the disciplinary components that initially were brought to bear, transdisciplinarity goes beyond disciplines. This is a feature which distinguishes transdisciplinary approaches from multi-disciplinary and interdisciplinary approaches. This is not to imply that individual researchers are able to completely disavow the assumptions, values and "lenses" of their disciplinary training; however, it does suggest that they can move beyond them by creating conceptual frameworks that transcend particular disciplines (Greckhamer et al. 2008).

Related to transcendence, or perhaps enabled by it, the concept of *emergence* is also an important principle of transdisciplinarity (see for example Austin et al. 2008; Jantsch 1972; Klein 2004; Steinmetz 2007). McMichael connects the idea of emergence to the implications of the prefix "trans" by beginning with a discussion of the word "transport" as

> a process of moving something across an intervening space, we now inhabit new boundaries; we move to a different plane.... Poets talk of "transports of delight"—our mind, our spirit, is transported to some new, exhilarating, romantic plane of experience. The idea of transportation accommodates this extra notion of an emergent experience, an emergent property. (2000, 204)

Emergence refers to more than one aspect of transdisciplinary research. First, the bringing in of multiple disciplinary perspectives and tools will allow a new approach to research to emerge. In other words, a conceptual and methodological framework for carrying out the research will be built; one that is different and larger than the sum of its parts. Second, new insights may emerge as a result of the research process; insights that would not have come forth without a transdisciplinary process. The idea of emergence speaks to the part of research practice that is unplanned, when unexpected pathways come into view, and when new insights are unearthed. In this regard, because transdisciplinary research projects are combining different bodies of knowledge and different methodological tools in service of addressing research topics holistically, one never knows what one will discover. Drawing on hybridity theory (discussed in chapter 2) some propose that transdisciplinarity creates a "third space" (Bhabba 1994) or "intermediate space" (Steinmetz 2007) that only emerges when disciplinary borders are crossed, eroded, and transcended (for example, see Steinmetz 2007). Drawing on Brandao (2007) Cameron and Mengler explain this as follows:

> Rather than "bridging" boundaries, transdisciplinarity denotes the transgression of boundaries, defining a space in between.... Transdisciplinarity is a system with no stable frontiers between disciplines, the concepts of order and disorder, the known and the unknown, rationality and imagination, conscious and unconscious, and the formal and informal. (2009, 194)

Similarly, Depres and colleagues (2004) suggest that transdisciplinarity creates a "mediation space" between disciplines in which all of the phases of research are played out, including the definition of problems, epistemological positions, concept selection, the development of a research strategy, the combining of research methods, and the development of theoretical frameworks.

Transdisciplinarity also necessitates *innovation* (Lawrence 2004; Van Manen 2001; Wickson et al. 2006). Researchers are building new conceptual structures, methodological frameworks, theoretical frameworks and strategies for evaluation. Because these projects are always issue- or problem-driven, those needs supersede disciplinary norms. All of this requires innovation which is linked to *flexibility*. When many different perspectives, sources of data and methodological tools are combined in new ways as each project demands, researchers must be flexible, open to new ideas, and willing to revise the conceptual and methodological framework as the process warrants. The research process is iterative, and so new insights may emerge and prompt changes throughout the process (this is reviewed in chapter 3).

Table 1.2 A Comparison of Multi-Disciplinarity, Interdisciplinarity and Transdisciplinarity

	Level of Collaboration between Disciplines
Multi-Disciplinarity	Collaboration between two or more disciplines without integration
Interdisciplinarity	Collaboration between two or more disciplines with varying levels of integration of concepts, theories, methods and findings
Transdisciplinarity	Collaboration between two or more disciplines with high levels of integration causing the development of new conceptual, theoretical and methodological frameworks

Disciplinarity and Transdisciplinarity: A Love-Hate Relationship

The quest for international security requires that each nation unconditionally surrenders some fraction of its liberty of action, of its sovereignty.

—Albert Einstein to Sigmund Freud (1932)

I think the biggest questions for many who are introduced to the idea of transdisciplinarity are: What about disciplines and disciplinary training? What is the relationship between disciplines and transdisciplinarity?

The questioning of disciplinary structures is scary and even threatening to many. The reasons for this are not difficult to understand. Wallerstein (2000) suggests that in the social sciences, for example, when disciplines were formed it became necessary to justify and maintain the boundaries (also see Greckhamer et al. 2008). Establishing boundaries is how professionals build their identities and claim their turf. It is important to bear in mind, however, that the development of university departments is the result of the institutionalization of knowledge-building—a process based on the distribution of rewards and resources and not necessarily "ideas." This is elaborated in the next chapter through the example of the institutionalization of Communications departments and again returned to in chapter 6 in a larger discussion of the academic career structure—the interconnected promotion, publication and funding systems.

Multi-disciplinary and interdisciplinary approaches to research leave the disciplinary production of knowledge intact. Transdisciplinarity, however, does provide an epistemological challenge to disciplinarity (Klein 2000, 2004; Newell 2000; Wickson et al. 2006). Nevertheless, while transdisciplinarity points to the limitations of disciplinary modes of knowledge production, it still relies on them. In other words, *the growth in transdisciplinarity does not mean the abandonment of disciplines.*

While it is true that some claim transdisciplinarity has the capability to make disciplines irrelevant (and as noted earlier, I think researchers should be free to view transdisciplinarity in different ways), most scholars suggest, and I concur, that a firm grounding in one's "home" discipline or disciplines is a vital asset in transdisciplinary research projects. In this regard, Giri writes: "Transdisciplinarity calls for an art of authentic embeddedness in one's discipline and transcendence does not mean cutting off from the ground where one stands but widening one's horizons…. There is a transdisciplinary undercurrent within each of our disciplines" (2002, 108). Klein (1990) similarly explains, and I strongly agree, that transdisciplinarity makes disciplines "instrumental to the larger framework" (Greckhamer et al. 2008, 313).

I propose that transdisciplinary researchers have to give up the idea that their disciplinary values and assumptions are "the truth" and instead become hyper-aware of their disciplinary lenses and then combine those perspectives with others, without privileging one way of looking at the issue over another. In this way, we can best serve our research agendas by drawing on the resources in our own disciplines as well as other relevant disciplines. The more important the research questions become in the contemporary world, the more we must commit ourselves to prioritizing answering them with all available tools.

In the beginning of this chapter I wrote: *Transdisciplinary research practices are issue- or problem-centered approaches to research that prioritize the problem at the center of research over discipline-specific concerns, theories or methods.* In order to elaborate on that rudimentary definition I suggest the following one as a broad, open and non-exclusive working understanding of transdisciplinarity: *Transdisciplinarity is a social justice oriented approach to research in which resources and expertise from multiple disciplines are integrated in order to holistically address a real-world issue or problem. Transdisciplinarity draws on knowledge from disciplines relevant to particular research issues or problems while ultimately transcending disciplinary borders and building a synergistic conceptual and methodological framework that is irreducible to the sum of its constituent parts. Transdisciplinarity views knowledge-building and dissemination as a holistic process and requires innovation and flexibility.*

With a working understanding of transdisciplinarity and how it differs from disciplinary, multi-disciplinary and interdisciplinary approaches to research, I move into a discussion of the academic and social context in which transdisciplinarity has emerged and in which it has become necessary.

Chapter Two

The Emergence of Transdisciplinary Research Practices

Conducting Social Research after the Social Justice Movements and in the Age of Globalization

The research system has become the trump card for the rich countries in global economic competition.

—Richard Worthington (2007, 476)

Transdisciplinary research practices have emerged within the context of a confluence of extraordinary changes within and beyond the academy. In a historical context these changes have occurred rapidly; however, they are manifold and have unfolded over the last several decades, culminating in the new research landscape. In order to understand the transdisciplinary paradigm it is important to consider: 1) the changing academic landscape, 2) the changing global context, and 3) the kinds of massive/complex problems humanity now faces and related changes in the public and public needs. Of course, these contexts overlap and intersect, with, for example, changes in the broader environment guiding changes within the academy. However, for the sake of explanation I, at times, separate changes within and beyond the academy. I first note the role of the social justice movements of the 1960s and 1970s in the development of critical theoretical traditions. Then I review broader issues related to globalization (including the development of hybrid theories and critical indigenous theories) and technological advances. Finally, I consider changes in the kinds of problems societies are now confronted with, as well as changes in the public's relationship to research. In all of these instances, the research community is responding to socio-histori-cal changes, as progressive and effective research communities do. As is often the case, when many in the research community are engaging with new theoretical and methodological questions, the cumulative impact of these efforts may go unidentified. It is the goal of this book to identify the larger shift in research practice.

Social Justice Movements, Theoretical Perspectives and Critical Area Studies

The social justice movements of the 1960s and 1970s—the women's movement (second wave feminism), the civil rights movement, the gay rights movement (all of which continue)—all sought social and politi-cal equality for groups marginalized based on status characteristics such as gender, race and sexual orientation. In essence, these movements exposed a range of widespread inequalities at the institutional level. By seeking to expose rampant inequalities and give marginalized groups a voice, the American landscape was altered significantly by the justice movements, the effects of which continue and which also prompted short and long-term changes within the research community. Women, people of color, and the sexually marginalized, formerly rendered invisible in social research, or included in ways that reified stereotypes and justi-fied relations of oppression, were sought out for meaningful inclusion in knowledge-building processes (Hesse-Biber & Leavy 2007). From the perspective of the research community, the cumulative impact of these movements has been a sustained reexamination of power within the knowledge-building process in order to avoid creating knowledge that is complicit in the oppression of minority groups (Hesse-Biber & Leavy 2011) and, later, in order to avoid research that exclusively promulgates a first-world perspective.

Feminist, Critical Race and Queer Theories

Feminist, critical race, and queer theories all emerged in multi- and interdisciplinary contexts and thus can not be claimed as the intellectual property of any one discipline. They are driven by social and political commitments. As fields of thought that emerged out of the justice move-ments they are all implicitly critical of existing knowledge structures. In this vein, all three theoretical traditions (which are umbrella terms for diverse bodies of theories) challenge formerly taken-for-granted dichotomies that shaped research practices and "common sense" thinking.

For example, feminist researchers have collectively challenged positivist conceptions of "objectivity" and called for a dismantling of the dualisms around which positivist science revolves: subject-object, rational-emotional, and concrete-abstract (Sprague & Zimmerman 1993)—dualisms which are now also challenged via transdisciplinarity. In this regard, feminists have argued that the positivist view of objectivity, primarily espoused in the quantitative paradigm, has produced a record of "scientific oppression"—relegating women, people of color, and sexual minorities to the category of "other" (Halpin 1989). Accordingly, researchers with feminist commitments have been at the forefront of theoretical and methodological challenges to positivism. A great deal of transdisciplinary scholarship reflects this work. In this regard, we can see how transdisciplinary enterprises produce their own synergistic theories and methodological principles—such as feminist standpoint epistemologies or theories of intersectionality, which are arguably transdisciplinary theoretical and methodological approaches to research.

Feminist, critical race, and queer theories share some overarching commonalities (despite the differences in their main foci: sexism/gender inequality, racism/racial inequality, and homophobia/inequalities based on sexual orientation and identity, respectively). All three theoretical frameworks share a social justice commitment to exposing and eradicating inequalities as well as a commitment to accessing subjugated perspectives. In terms of accessing subjugated knowledges, these perspectives also value experiential knowledge, and they seek to avoid essentialist categories that erase differences. In this vein, over the past two decades all three bodies of theoretical thought have trended towards theories of intersectionality that take seriously the interconnections between gender, race and sexual orientation. Researchers must therefore be attentive to overlapping and even conflicting identities (Ritzer 2008) [see Patricia Hill-Collins 1991 for a full discussion of intersectionality theory]. Further, the nature of "concealable identities" (Faulkner 2006)—those identities that can be disclosed or hidden in different contexts such as sexual orientation or religion—may also propel new conceptualizations of intersectionality theory. Given the complexity around "identity" from this perspective, transdisciplinary approaches to research, which embrace messiness and paradox, are often useful in projects informed by intersectionality theories and may produce additional theories.

Additionally, these perspectives all view status characteristics (such as gender, race and sexual orientation) as socially constructed. In this regard, the social construction of gender is assumed across feminist perspectives (Glenn 2000). This means that gender differs from biological sex. Most simply, gender is a set of historically and culturally specific ideas attributed to males and females that are used within a society to signify masculinity and femininity (see Lorber 1993, 2008). There is nothing natural about social constructions; they are created and deployed within power-rich environments. Similarly, critical race theory posits that race is a set of historically and culturally specific ideas about race that are linked to skin color but are not its equivalent. Critical race theory explains that racism is insidious and normalized (Hesse-Biber & Leavy 2011; Ritzer, 2008). In this vein, critical race theory investigates "hierarchical racial structures of society" (Denzin 2005, 279). Delgado and Stefancic (2001) suggest that dominant groups racialize different minority groups at different historical moments as a result of changes in social, material and/ or symbolic contexts (Hesse-Biber & Leavy 2011). For example, Delgado and Stefancic note that white America racialized Arabs as terrorists after September 11, 2001.

By breaking down artificial dualisms, complicating the concept of identity, and putting a spotlight on the issue of power in the research process, these critical theories have informed transdisciplinarity in diverse contexts.

Postmodern, Post-structural and Post-colonial Theories

Postmodern, post-structural and post-colonial theoretical perspectives are all hyper-attentive to how power informs the research process. As such, these perspectives all critique traditional, positivist approaches to research and the grand theories such approaches espouse and validate.

The postmodern era is frequently characterized by an explosion of media forms, the fragmentation of history, transnational capitalism, and technological changes (that change modern conceptions of time and space) (Hesse-Biber & Leavy 2011). Postmodern theory is an umbrella term for a diverse body of theories that attend to these changes.

A postmodern perspective conceptualizes research as a "knowledge-building *process*." Knowledge is not discovered (as positivism suggests) but is rather built out of a power-laden research process (Hesse-Biber &

Leavy 2011). In this vein, postmodern theory rejects totalizing or grand theories and absolute truths in favor of partial and situated "truths" (a multiplicity of context-dependent truths) (see Haraway 1991). Postmodern theory accounts for the sociopolitical nature of experience and rejects essentialist identity categories that erase differences. Postmodern theories have prompted much more attention to methodological practices of reflexivity throughout the knowledge-building process. Therefore, postmodern theory poses a major challenge to traditional models of knowledge production—a challenge which transdisciplinary researchers are taking on.

Post-structuralism is also an umbrella category for diverse theoretical work. Post-structuralist pioneer Jacques Derrida (1966) proposed a method of critical deconstruction where unities are broken down (for example grand theories or discourses) in order to investigate what they exclude, what they silence. With the goal of disrupting dominant knowledges (Riger 1992, 735) or "jamming the theoretical machinery" (Irigaray 1985, 78), researchers informed by post-structural theories attempt to expose and subvert oppressive relations of power through these practices. As the turn to transdisciplinarity suggests, the magnitude of contemporary problems and challenges makes this work quite important.

Post-colonialism is another power-attentive critical perspective. In essence, post-colonial theories seek to recognize and cease to replicate relations of colonization in knowledge-building practices. In her pioneering work on developing a "methodology of the oppressed" Chela Sandoval explains the term post-colonial as "a utopian site located somewhere beyond authoritarianism and domination" (2000, 185). As globalizing processes have increased, critical indigenous theories have been built, and transnational first world-third world research collaborations have been forged. Post-colonial theories have aided in the development of transdisciplinarity.

Embodiment Theory

Embodiment theory[1] has also emerged in recent decades out of feminism, psychoanalysis and phenomenology. This theoretical perspective focuses on the body—how bodies are conceptualized, controlled, experienced; how they move in time and space, and so forth.

Elizabeth Grosz (1995) distinguishes "inscriptive" and "the lived body" approaches to embodiment research. The inscribed body serves as a site where social meanings are created and resisted. Influenced by the work of Foucault (1976) and Bordo (1989), Grosz writes: "The body is not outside of history, for it is produced through and in history" (1994, 148). For example, the way we sex or gender or race the body is deeply implicated in existing relations of power (pp. 141–2).

In embodiment scholarship "the lived body" refers to people's experiential knowledge. Grosz is influenced by Merleau-Ponty (1962) who posited we must look at the "necessary interconnectedness" of the mind and body (Grosz 1994, 86). He argued that experience exists between the mind and body (Merleau-Ponty 1962). Therefore, the body is not viewed as an object but rather as the "condition and context" through which social actors have relations to objects and through which they give and receive information (Grosz 1994, 86). Put simply, the body is a tool through which meaning is created. Based on her research on the bodily experience of pregnancy, Spry (2006) suggests that in order to access experiential knowledge researchers must find ways to access "enfleshed knowledge." This is a holistic view of experience, conceptualizing experience as inseparable from its bodily components. This view also affirms that the mind and body are intimately interconnected. These advances in our understanding of embodiment and the physicality of experience, which have largely emerged in theoretical scholarship, serve as a part of the context for various transdisciplinary methodological innovations (such as many arts-based research practices).

All of these theoretical perspectives—feminism, critical race theory, queer theory, postmodern, post-structural, post-colonial and embodiment theory—attend to issues of power and have caused a significant renegotiation and elaboration of the ways in which research is conceptualized and carried out. All of these perspectives suggest a holistic and process-oriented view of knowledge-building. Moreover, they all emphasize reflexivity and by extension highlight issues of ethics and knowledge-building. Finally, they all expose issues of inequality which raises questions about research and the public good. Also, emphasizing diversity and experiential knowledge, these theoretical perspectives help pave the way for participatory transdisciplinary approaches to research.

Fields Built out of Critique

The collective impact of the social justice movements and new theoretical traditions they have inspired has been the emergence of a range of "area studies." These emergent fields have developed in necessarily multi-disciplinary and interdisciplinary contexts. Moreover, these are "fields forged in critique" (Klein 2000)—critiquing both conventional, power-laden knowledge-building practices and the social inequalities those practices help to justify and maintain. Further, these fields are all social justice oriented. These area studies or fields include Black studies, Chicano/Chicana studies, cultural studies, future studies, and women's studies/gender studies. The emergence of these fields has caused the creation of new programs, departments, programming and research institutions as well as new publications, conferences and organizations across the academic landscape, and consequently new ways of thinking about and conducting social research. However, there has also been a cumulative impact from these area studies—now widely accepted as legitimate knowledge domains. There has been a transcendence of the "incubation" phase of these fields as they have gained legitimacy in the academy; now we are at the phase of considering the effects of these programs on knowledge-building practices overall, across the academy. Most notably, disciplines across the academy have been impacted by multi- and interdisciplinary fields, and the light they shine on practices of knowledge production (Johnson 2001). In other words, multi-disciplinarity and interdisciplinarity have impacted disciplinarity creating something new—a "third space"—transdisciplinarity.

Let's take the example of cultural studies for illustrative purposes. Cultural studies began as an international groundswell in the academy based on a critique of how power informs knowledge-building. The term itself was only coined in 1964 with the movement taking off from the 1970–1990s. Despite the fairly recent emergence of cultural studies, at this point two important changes within the academy are clear.

First, cultural studies is now a distinct academic field or area study. Accordingly, the field has been institutionalized. For example, many institutions have cultural studies departments or programs and journals, organizations and conferences devoted to cultural studies abound.

Second, the content of cultural studies (emergent theory and empirical research) has impacted knowledge-production across academic/research institutions. In his analysis of the impact of cultural studies programs Johnson explains this as follows:

> I have reached for a new term—"transdisciplinary"—because the old terms—"interdisciplinary," "multidisciplinary," etc.—do not express the

fact that our disciplines now share something new. They share the effects of the cultural studies intervention itself, many common paradigms, debates and issues, and the more general "cultural turn." (2001, 262)

Johnson goes on to note the three key moments in these "cross-disciplinary dynamics": "1) Cultural studies borrows from adjacent disciplines, 2) these same and other disciplines reappropriate some elements which cultural studies has transformed, 3) the distinctive transdisciplinary moment, of *shared but different* discourses on the cultural" (2001, 271).

The example of cultural studies illustrates how a transdisciplinary enterprise can develop within the academy, and how in turn, the transdisciplinary project continues to impact research practices across the disciplines. Again, transdisciplinary enterprises may produce synergistic theoretical and methodological practices that are then used and adapted across area studies. Black studies, Chicano/Chicana studies, future studies, and women's studies/gender studies have also impacted academia (and research processes) in these ways. So, for example, the women's movement and feminist theories influence research practice well beyond "women's studies." Across the contexts in which transdisciplinarity is practiced, social justice values and goals underscore research projects.

The Institutionalization of Multi- and Interdisciplinary Fields: Communications Departments

While the spread of cultural studies and women's studies interdisciplinary programs remains an ongoing process, the institutionalization of communications departments is now taken for granted. A brief look at the emergence of communications departments shows both how the academic landscape can shift and how transdisciplinarity can become normative. In the United States communications studies did not fully emerge as a discipline until the 1960s; becoming normative within the academy by the 1970s and 1980s. Communication studies grew out of speech and rhetoric departments, theatre departments, and social science departments including anthropology, political science, psychology and sociology. All of these distinct departments partially focused on strains of what came to be termed "communication studies." As a way of restructuring academic departments, communications became institutionalized as a distinctive discipline and is now widely accepted as an institutionalized part of the academic landscape. Although housed across the academy as "departments" and not "programs" (as is usually the case with other interdisciplinary fields such as cultural studies and women's studies), communications departments house multidisciplinary scholars with backgrounds in the humanities and social sciences. Scholars working in this tradition may employ research methods that developed in specific social science disciplines; however, the necessarily multidisciplinary origins of communications have led to the development of new research questions and new approaches to research aimed at answering those questions. The merging of multiple sets of disciplinary resources around a particular set of research interests has therefore produced new synergistic methods and theories. Moreover, communications departments have been influenced by the fields forged in critique noted earlier, and are also influenced by those interventions. This too has fueled the creation of new approaches to research that may be transdisciplinary in nature.

Far-Reaching Changes in Knowledge-Building

When considering the impact of the social justice movements, critical and other non-disciplinary theoretical developments and the emergence of critical area studies (and corresponding changes in the academic/research landscape) it is important to explore the broad-based cumulative impact on knowledge-building. Gibbons, Limoges, Nowotny, Schwartzmann, Scott and Trow map out these issues in *The New Production of Knowledge: The Dynamics of Science and Research in Contemporary Societies* (1994) in which they detail a new mode of research based on transdisciplinarity, heterogeneity and reflexivity (a power-attentive practice). They summarize the major shifts in knowledge-building/research practices as follows:

> From simplicity to complexity
>
> From singularity to heterogeneity and hybridity
>
> From linearity to non-linearity
>
> From unity and universality to unifying and integrative processes
>
> From fragmentation to connection, collaboration and consequence
>
> From boundary formation to blurring and crossing
>
> From the short-term and the ephemeral to the long-term
>
> From analysis and reduction to synthesis and dialogue.
>
> (Klein 2000, 12)

By looking at these larger changes in the social and academic landscapes, the backdrop in which transdisciplinarity emerged becomes clearer. It is now equally important to consider how globalization (and related theoretical work) has fuelled transdisciplinary vision.

A Globalizing World

Globalization is a dialectical process involving economic, political and cultural exchanges. Herath (2008) suggests that globalization is "a process [that] contributes to a shrinking of time and space" (p. 821). Although globalization is far more complex than will be discussed here, three major domains of globalization are: 1) transnational capitalism, 2) development (including unequal development, sustainable development and ecological concerns), and 3) cultural exchange. A range of issues relating to transnational capitalism and development—both of which can be categorized as material aspects of globalization—has emerged as Western and non-Western perspectives/interests bump up against each other in a world of shifting but starkly unequal relations of power. Concurrently, a range of issues related to cultural globalization—which can be categorized as the symbolic and ritual aspects of globalization—has emerged as these dialectical processes occur causing the displacing, transplanting, morphing, and reifying of local cultural discourses within a changing landscape.

In the globalizing world, geographic and cultural borders are shifting, and individuals and groups may respond to these fluctuating borders through (re)negotiating collective identities (Leavy 2008). In this regard, shifting borders can both reaffirm and alter group identities as cultural and spatial borders shift and overlap in new ways (Leavy 2008).

Globalization and Hybridity

In a world of rapidly shifting borders hybrid theories posit that the concept of national identity itself is based on an idea of an "imagined community" (Anderson 1991; Bhabba 1990; Iyall Smith & Leavy 2008). Hybridity refers to the merging of cultural forms that create something new. Bhabba (1994) refers to this as a "third space." With a marked increase in multidisciplinary studies of globalization (which are of course a response to globalizing processes), theoretical and empirical work on hybridity has been rapidly increasing over the past few decades. Hybridity scholarship "draws on hybrid, post-colonial, critical race, and feminist theories in order to interrogate the complex processes of identity construction and meaning-making prevalent in the globalizing world. Using data derived largely on the micro level, scholars are conducting research that links 'the particular' and 'the universal' in multidirectional ways" (Leavy 2008, 167, drawing on Iyall Smith 2008). In this way researchers are linking the micro and macro levels and the concrete and abstract in complex ways.

Hybridity research focuses on the relationship between identity and context. As I noted in a volume on hybridity, "Studies of hybrid identities center on the dialectical and mutually productive relationship between a multiplicity of hybridized identities in a shifting, globalizing context" (Leavy 2008, 167). Hybridity researchers ask: "How do different groups, confronted with specific and diverse cultural forces, economic forces, and institutional settings, negotiate identity and cultural space within this context? In what ways are the cultural spaces created by the fissures between, and fusing of, divergent cultural elements in fact *productive spaces* in which identities are constructed and contested?" (Leavy 2008, 167).

Hybridity scholarship has also emerged out of interdisciplinary fields built out of critique, an academic trend noted earlier. For example, some of the most important borderlands work has developed out of Chicano/Chicana identity studies. Anzaldua's pioneering work (1987) extended our understanding of borders far beyond geographic space, as she noted the Mexico-US border is a "vague and undetermined place created by the emotional residue of an unnatural boundary" (1987, 3). Further, Anzaldua noted that within this context, "plural personalities" emerge, thus producing more heterogeneity as people learn to "juggle cultures" (1987, 79). The question for the research community becomes: how do you access these new phenomena? Transdisciplinarity is a response to these needs. Robertson (1996) notes that the issue of "globality" has necessarily changed how researchers think about "disciplinary boundaries" (p. 127). He goes on to explain that a global perspective requires "critical disciplinary mutations" (1996, 127). In this regard, Perrig-Chiello and Darbellay (2002) posit that transdisciplinarity is a global perspective that "re-organises disciplinary knowledge in order to solve a complex problem" (p. 24).

As globalizing processes continue to rapidly transform issues of place, space and identity, hybridity research will continue to emerge (Leavy, 2008). Historically most hybridity research projects have been designed to employ conventional disciplinary research methods such as interviews, ethnography and historical comparative methods. As I noted in an earlier work, our more sophisticated understanding of hybridity will allow us to formulate new research questions that require new research practices (Leavy 2008). I now suggest that this methodological innovation is occurring as a result of developments in critical indigenous studies and related transdisciplinary practices. Nicolescu (2002) posits that transdisciplinarity is "intrinsically global in character" (p. 3). Globalizing processes will only increase; therefore, the transnational research community will need to continue developing tools suitable for empirical investigations of hybridity, theory-building, and related research topics. Robertson suggests that "the debate about globality is leading... to a revamping of the matrix of disciplines and perhaps, in the long run, an end to disciplinarity as we know it" (1996, 128).

Critical Indigenous Theories

Critical approaches to indigenous inquiry have been generated since the 1990s as a result of the evolution of the theoretical approaches to flow from the justice movements coupled with the effects of globalizing processes on the transnational research community. These approaches also draw from some of the methodological genres reviewed in this book, including arts-based and community-based research practices. Denzin and Lincoln (2008) write: "Critical indigenous inquiry begins with the concerns of indigenous people. It is assessed in terms of the benefits it creates for them" (p. 2). In the context of research projects, these approaches aim to access the subjugated knowledges of indigenous people for social justice purposes determined, at least partly, by research participants (and non-Western researchers). In terms of renegotiating research practices more broadly, critical indigenous inquiry "embraces the commitment by indigenous scholars to decolonize Western methodologies, to criticize and demystify the ways in which Western science and the modern academy have been part of the colonial apparatus" (Denzin & Lincoln 2008, 2). This requires a systematic questioning and renegotiating of conventional models of knowledge production. Robertson urges us to consider how viewing globalization as a part of all social research practice (and not a sub-discipline or specialization) "involves the questioning of the entire intellectual apparatus of the social sciences" (1996, 128). In this effort

Denzin and Lincoln (2008) advocate a "borderland epistemology" (p. 2) which I argue is necessarily a transdisciplinary grounding. Transdisciplinary visions (and practices) are needed to meet the demands of critical indigenous theoretical advancements.

Technological Advancements

Technological advances have also greatly aided the development of transdisciplinary innovations. With respect to transdisciplinary research, technological progress has been vital in three primary ways: 1) altering the global landscape in ways that become the subjects of scientific study, 2) creating transnational communities and enabling transnational research collaborations, and 3) prompting methodological innovation/allowing for the construction and rapid dissemination of multi-media texts.

Technological changes have altered the global landscape in both universal and locally particular ways. Primary examples with respect to scientific inquiry include but are not limited to: the first-world/third-world technological divide; environmental issues (and related ethical issues with respect to the disposing of toxic materials in poor areas); changes in education; economic changes (the flow of capital, personal and professional money-management, changes in the labor force); changes in personal/social networking practices; and changes in communication practices at the individual, community, national and transnational levels. These issues and others have become topics of scientific investigation.

With respect to the creation of transnational communities and transnational research collaborations, I begin with the former. The "World Wide Web" has allowed for the creation of "virtual communities"—thereby changing traditional conceptions of what community means.[2] Virtual communities are connected via technological means; they exist in "cyberspace." These communities themselves have become the focus of much social research. As these networks continue to develop across national borders, facilitating social action research on a new scale, the research community will continue to explore these issues. High speed and cost effective communications technologies have also allowed for the building of transnational research communities. This is one of the most historically important and promising developments in the research community, allowing for the transnational and transdisciplinary sharing of information, methodological strategies, research findings, and non-indigenous concerns.

Finally, new technologies have allowed for the construction, preservation and dissemination of many new kinds of "texts." Examples of relevant technologies include the Internet, Photoshop, digital cameras, digital imaging technology and sound files. There is also a range of "participatory media" and "interactive media" (Cameron & Mengler 2009). These technologies allow the broader research community to produce and publish textual forms that would not have been possible before, the importance of which is highlighted in later discussions of community-based research and arts-based research.

Researchers suggest that transdisciplinarity is necessary for addressing the new and complex problems emerging from economic and technical globalization (including related social, cultural and political impacts) (Thompson et al. 2001, 25).

Problems and the Public

Transdisciplinarity is an issue- or problem-centered approach to research. Multiple sets of disciplinary resources and/or expertise are brought together for the purpose of serving the project at hand: building a conceptual, methodological and theoretical framework that can best address the issue or problem under investigation. Accordingly, the nature of the problems demanding attention from the research community drives transdisciplinarity.

Complex and Diffuse Issues/Problems

We live in an increasingly complex world, which Cameron and Mengler (2009) refer to as a "hyper-complex world." The problems facing humanity are enormous, complex and diffuse. Some of the greatest challenges include, but are not limited to, the environmental crisis, sustainability, epidemic health problems (such as cancer), violence (in many forms), starkly inequitable development (and other economic inequalities), educational crises (including inequalities in education and other social inequalities), to name but a few. No one discipline has met or can meet the challenges of contemporary society.

For example, the urgent issue of creating a comprehensive approach to sustainability highlights the need for transdisciplinarity (and the inherent transdisciplinary character of many contemporary problems). McMichael notes: "The links between human society and the natural world are fundamental to exploration of this topic—which would therefore be jeopardized by continuation of the historical epistemological rupture between the social and natural sciences" (2001, 208). Sumi (2000) urges that we must create a sustainability science because humanity can not stay on the present course. To do so we need an issue-driven, transdisciplinary approach that holistically addresses the need for balance or synergy among the three subsystems of our environment: 1) the global natural system (climate), 2) the socioeconomic system, and 3) the human system (level of groups and individuals) (Sumi 2000). Sumi further explains the components of these systems as follows: 1) the global natural system includes the climate system, energy and resources, and the ecosystem; 2) the socioeconomic system includes the economy, politics, industry and technology; and 3) the human system includes security/safety, lifestyle, health, norms and values (2000, 169). A host of complex problems and issues directly call for a *synergistic analysis* of these varied dimensions of our environment. Such issues and problems include, but are not limited to, climate change, infectious disease, natural disasters, mass production, consumption and destruction (Sumi 2000).

There are numerous other examples of research topics that demand transdisciplinarity. For example, McMichael notes that the topics of urbanization and the mass production of automobiles raise a host of issues including, but not restricted to, air pollution (and many related health and environmental problems), lack of exercise (linked to obesity rates, health issues, identity/esteem issues, and other issues of daily life such as media use), traffic and road rage (linked to larger issues of violence), and the fragmentation of neighborhoods (with related issues pertaining to social class, race and defacto segregation) (2001, 209). Therefore, no one disciplinary perspective can possibly address these issues alone—not effectively. Disciplinary resources need to be pooled with new resources and frameworks generated as a result. There are many other *necessarily* transdisciplinary issues that will be discussed in depth in this book, such as violence and health.

The Moral Imperative

There is a moral imperative driving the need for transdisciplinary approaches to real-world issues of import. To say that transdisciplinarity is a social justice oriented perspective is not simply to give lip service to the movements of the past. The problems and issues at the center of transdisciplinary efforts demand attention from those best equipped to provide solutions to the challenges of contemporary life: the research community. As knowledge-producers we have a moral and ethical obligation to use all available tools for addressing pressing social needs. Ernst (2008) implores researchers to consider both their obligation to the public good and their obligation to educate the researchers and leaders of tomorrow so that they can continue to meet new challenges. He writes: "We academics are obliged to develop wisdom for comprehending the transdisciplinary and trans-cultural connections that provide clues for solving the major pending problems" (2008, 121). Ernst goes on to explain that knowledge is a necessary supportive base for wisdom but not its equivalent. Wisdom requires a broad view and the "comprehension of connectivity" (2008, 123). Moreover, wisdom can be employed with compassion (Ernst, 2008), which is a necessary dimension of social justice practices. He further suggests, and I concur, that the academic/research community has to function *within* society (p. 129). He writes: "We do not need mere experts knowing everything about very little. Encyclopedic knowledge is better stored in databases. Society is in need of innovative and initiative citizens who are ready to assume responsibility" (2008, 129). Researchers can develop transdisciplinary visions and corresponding approaches to social research in order to better serve public interests; in order to be *useful*.[3]

The Engaged Public

In recent years there have been significant moves by the research community towards public scholarship; transdisciplinarity advances this agenda. In order to address real-world issues and problems, and better serve public interests, researchers need to seriously engage with individuals and groups outside of academia. For example, even identifying research topics that can serve "public interests" may need to be a process that occurs between researchers and other relevant groups.

Many scholars note that in recent years the public has become more educated and more engaged in social issues/problems (perhaps in part due to the magnitude of those issues and problems and increased access to information via the Internet and other media) (for example, see Russell et al. 2008). Like others, I suggest that while the public (particularly in the West) has become engaged, many are also disenchanted with the ability of major institutions (political, economic, scientific) to deal with the ever-increasing scope of "urgent" issues. In short, the public may have more interest but less faith. This is precisely why academic/research institutions need to actively respond to what is happening in the world, and not to try to remain detached and outside of those realities. Russell and colleagues (2008) suggest that the "engaged populace" is a primary driver of transdisciplinarity (and, I would add, an asset, a resource). They suggest there is a growing public demand to be included in scientific practices and for the scientific community to seek a "shared vision" or "contract" with the public (2008, 464). I suggest research must occur both within and outside of the academy (including groups and interests beyond the academy but not become beholden to any one set of interests). Transdisciplinarity is problem-centered, or what Russell and colleagues call a collaborative method of "responsive problem-solving" and therefore "has much promise in bringing universities into line with the new knowledge landscape and in meeting global challenges of the 21st century" (2008, 461).

The following table summarizes the primary changes to the academic landscape and how they have impacted the development of transdisciplinary research practice.

Table 2.1 Summary of Changes to Social Research Landscape

Change	Primary Location	Primary Effect
Critical theoretical perspectives, area studies, and the institutionalization of multi- and interdisciplinary departments	Within academy	Creates pathways and synergies across disciplines for transdisciplinary collaboration
Globalization and corresponding economic, development, cultural and technological changes	The globalizing world	Creates the means for transnational research collaborations and diverse strategies for communicating research findings
Increasing public awareness of significant and multi-dimensional contemporary challenges	Public	Creates an ethical substructure for research and a practical imperative

Research Topics

The factors that lead to the cultivation of transdisciplinarity also influence the kinds of topics transdisciplinary approaches are generally used to study. For example, some topics currently receiving a great deal of attention in transdisciplinary research include, but are not limited to, sustainability, health, education, violence, obesity, (un)employment, inequality in a global context, and identity in a global context. For the remainder of this book I draw on examples pertaining to the social world (and not "life world" topics more generally, such as environmental sustainability, as has been the case in much of the transdisciplinary literature to date due to projects originating in the natural sciences, environmental sciences and medicine). I use examples that are most likely to originate in the social sciences, education and health care. For example, I review how transdisciplinary approaches can be used in studies on gender inequality, preventive health care, obesity and violence. To do so, in the following chapter I review general research design issues one might consider as one builds a transdisciplinary project. In the next two chapters I review two major genres of transdisciplinary research: community-based research and arts-based research. In the final chapter I discuss issues pertaining to evaluation in this emerging paradigm. I also suggest how the community might move forward in cultivating transdisciplinarity as a problem-solving tool.

Chapter Three

Research Design

Issue- or Problem-Centered Approaches

Transdisciplinarity is not a vehicle that we deploy to stay alive or accomplish our projects. It is a way of being alive. It counsels us to relativize our own understandings, to rearrange our prejudices, to undermine the very knowledge that gives us a presumptive leg-up of expertise on others, to seek to recombine one's "can't helps," and to decenter oneself and seek the marginal.

—Macdonald (2000, 244)

Transdisciplinary approaches to research can be used to study a vast range of research topics, designed in creative ways, and may draw on expertise in any combination of disciplines. Moreover, transdisciplinary research designs may employ any methods in pursuit of the research objectives. Any research method, qualitative, quantitative, hybrid, or a multi-method or mixed method strategy may be used in transdisciplinary research. Some researchers may even create new methods to address their research questions. Methods are simply tools for data collection (Hesse-Biber & Leavy 2011) and do not dictate whether or not the approach to research is transdisciplinary. In short, *there are no standard templates of what transdisciplinary research should look like or what steps it must follow.* Nevertheless, the principles and goals of transdisciplinary research offer suggestions for how to build a research design that meets the goals of any particular project, while maximizing transdisciplinarity. I begin this chapter by reviewing some of the general issues to consider when developing a transdisciplinary project. Then I provide an in-depth discussion of research design broken down into three stages: 1) planning; 2) data collection; and 3) analysis, interpretation and representation.

Problem-Centered Research and "Responsive Methodologies"

To begin, transdisciplinary research is necessarily issue- or problem-centered. This means that all design issues are determined in relation to the specific issue or problem at hand. *The development of a research strategy is driven by the research topics and purpose(s).* Wickson and colleagues (2006) speak to the design implications of a problem-centered approach to research by asserting that transdisciplinary research "is characterized by an interpenetration of epistemologies in the development of methodology.... The dissolution of disciplinary boundaries is necessary for the construction of novel or unique methodologies tailored to the problem and its context" (p. 1050). This means that there is a limitless pool of possible combinations of disciplinary knowledges, design features and methods choices. Further, design strategies are not built around researchers' preferences, guiding assumptions, and the like, but rather, around how to best address the research problem.

Of course researchers do bring their disciplinary assumptions to bear on the research process, and this can be used to strengthen the research, not weaken it. In order to get the most out of disciplinary expertise while maximizing transdisciplinarity each researcher must engage in a reflexive process where he or she becomes aware of his or her assumptions and is willing to question and challenge them. Moreover, the researcher or research team must pull in needed expertise, including literature from other relevant fields, and collaborators when appropriate.

Although every project will be structured differently, the research strategy developed for a transdisciplinary project should involve a holistic approach to the research purpose and questions. In other words, it should consider "the whole." This means that the research strategy should take into account as much of the issue or problem at hand as is researchable in a given study, and consider the problem or issue from multiple vantage points or perspectives. As you design a study continually reflect on questions like:

- What is being left out of this design?

- What am I missing, failing to get at, failing to see?
- What perspectives are not being considered?
- Are there other ways to look at these issues?
- Have I brought in the relevant bodies of disciplinary/interdisciplinary knowledge?
- Have key concepts been defined using multiple disciplinary and cultural lenses?
- Am I continually approaching this with a transdisciplinary orientation?

When thinking about "the whole" a helpful example comes from the practice of "integrative health care" which is also termed "holistic," "humanistic" and "whole client" health care (Klein 2000). Integrative health care is a transdisciplinary approach to health care that takes biological, social, psychological and ethical factors into account (Klein 2000). Klein explains "integrative health care" as follows: "The human being is perceived as an interacting, integrated whole. Correspondingly, treatment is framed as a dynamic and fluid response and, finally, the health-care team constitutes an interacting partnership of professionals who treat the client as a whole" (2000, 56). In other words, historically healthcare has emerged out of the natural sciences and emphasized biological and physiological wellness. However, researchers are now turning to more holistic approaches to health that integrate the natural sciences and the social/behavioral sciences and thus require transdisciplinarity (Piko & Kopp 2008).

Piko and Kopp (2008) provide an excellent empirical example of a transdisciplinary approach to health research that occurred in Hungary. In the 1980s Hungary had the lowest life expectancy and highest mortality rate in Europe (Piko & Kopp 2008). A transdisciplinary research team assembled in order to study the "health status" of Hungarian populations. Social/behavioral researchers from the following fields were included and categorized under the umbrella term "Behavioral Medicine": medical psychology, medical sociology, medical anthropology, medical communications studies and medical ethics (Piko & Kopp 2008). The multi-method projects involved three stages: "a research phase, measuring the health status of the population; an educational phase, applying research results in the courses for medical and other health science students; and a practice phase, developing skills and prevention programmes based on the research results" (Piko & Kopp 2008, 306). As this example illustrates, moves towards integrated or holistic approaches to health care promote rich transdisciplinarity.

Another interesting example of moving from disciplinarity to transdisciplinarity comes from the field of architecture. John Last (2000) has written about his engagement with transdisciplinarity throughout his career, although he hadn't always named it as such. He writes about a public health course for architects as a necessary and necessarily transdisciplinary part of training.

> Ventilation, lighting, heating and cooling, water purification, sanitary services, sewerage... describe the relationship between housing conditions and mental health... "ekistics"—science and art of making cities and towns aesthetically, socially, psychologically, and spiritually pleasing to live in as well as healthy and functionally efficient. (Last 2000, 194)

This is another example of thinking about "the whole" through transdisciplinarity.

Moreover, the research design strategy itself should be holistic. A *holistic approach to research design* means that each phase of the research should be integrated with the other phases (Hesse-Biber & Leavy 2011). Wickson and colleagues suggest three dimensions of integration: 1) integrating epistemologies, 2) theory and practice, and 3) researcher and the context of research. This is a *synergistic approach* to research methodology. As opposed to a set of linear steps researchers may follow, a holistic or synergistic research design might look very different, with periods of cycling back, re-testing or re-questioning, making modifications to the design based on new insights, and so forth. Transdisciplinarity therefore requires *an evolving methodology* that follows an *iterative or responsive process* where the methodology evolves over the course of the research process as a result of new learning (Wickson et al. 2006). Interestingly, this positions researchers, and rightfully so, as learners in the research process and not all-knowing experts who can design "perfect" research studies without actually collecting and looking at context specific data—which is often the case in traditional disciplinary research. Transdisciplinary research presupposes that researchers don't necessarily know everything they should be asking or doing until they are in the process, learning. If we had all of the answers we wouldn't need to do research.

Again, the key principle of *flexibility* comes to bear. Research strategies must be flexible enough to allow for adaptation to new insights[1] (Russell et al. 2008). Therefore, transdisciplinary research follows "responsive method-ologies" (Wickson et al. 2006). Wickson and colleagues define a responsive methodology as "iterative and an ongoing part of the research process… evolving methodology" (p. 1051). In this regard Flinterman and associ-ates (2001) suggest a *spiral model of research design*[2] as follows: "1) define research field, 2) identify relevant actors, 3) literature search, 4) preliminary data (in-depth interviews, focus groups, discussion groups/workshops), 5) feedback by all (and repetition), 6) develop shared vision/plan of action" (Flinterman et al. 2001, 259–260).

This procedure can be used to "identify, assess, and prioritize research topics; to formulate research questions and objectives; to design research projects; and to analyze and interpret research results in a trans-disciplinary manner (Flinterman et al. 2001, 259). This model can be adapted to suit particular projects. It is very important to emphasize that the model suggested by Flinterman and colleagues is just one example of what a responsive methodology may look like. This model should not be taken as "the" way to conduct transdisciplinary research—there is no one-size-fits-all strategy.

A responsive approach (or spiral approach) to research design follows *the principle of recursiveness*. Recursiveness is a key feature that strength-ens the quality of transdisciplinary research (and as noted in chapter 6, is central to issues of evaluation) (Pohl et al. 2007). Recursiveness is another way of describing an iterative research process, where the researcher(s) cycle back to check data as they go and adapt to new insights. Pohl and colleagues write:

> Recursiveness (or iteration) implies foreseeing that project steps may be repeated several times in case of need. The possible limitation or uncertainty of a preliminary result thus becomes a means of targeted learning. Recursiveness is important in all phases of the research pro-cess. (2007, 22–23)

By applying the principle of recursiveness researchers avoid rigid research strategies in favor of a living research design that is influenced and strengthened by additional learning. Krimsky (2000) offers another way to think about this by suggesting that a transdisciplinary approach to methodology requires *recurring* communication, critique, disclosure, evaluation and reporting. Pohl and colleagues expand on their discussion of recursiveness as follows: "A recursive design is a meaningful pragmatic way of working with intermediary results and further developing them with the help of critical assessment" (Pohl et al. 2007, 43). This suggests that recursiveness is a way of enacting reflexivity (Pohl et al. 2007).

While reflexivity has been a major buzz word in the qualitative research community for the past few decades, there is far more attention paid to its philosophical importance than to how one actually "does" reflexivity. By adopting an iterative research process researchers are able to put the principles of reflexivity into practice along with flexibility and innovation. McMichael posits that transdisciplinarity requires an "open, flexible, and self-reflective framework" (2000, 218). So while transdisciplinary research projects may look very different from each other—appearing in different "shapes"—they share holistic and synergistic approaches, they require flexibility and innovation and typically follow a responsive methodology of some sort that fosters reflexivity.

Table 3.1 Summary of Holistic and Responsive Approach

Holistic Approach to Research Design

1. Considers problem holistically (comprehensively, as a whole)
2. Holistic or synergistic research process (all phases integrated with each other)

Evolving or Responsive Methodology

1. Iterative process with periods of cycling back
2. Follows principle of recursiveness
3. Continual process of adapting to new learning requires flexibility and innovation
4. Process requires recurring communication/reflection and thus fosters reflexivity

---

Research Design: Planning

As reviewed, research design decisions should be made in relation to the research topic, purpose and questions. A problem-centered approach to research design implies that "the order of the phases and the amount of resources dedicated to each phase depend on the kind of problem under investigation and on the state of knowledge" (Hadorn et al. 2008,

19). Wickson and colleagues (2006) suggest considering the following design features as you develop a project (although this is not meant to be prescriptive):

1. responsive goals (refining and shifting goals)
2. broad preparation (theory and literature from multiple disciplines)
3. evolving methodology
4. significant outcome (contribute to the solution of a problem, "satisfying multiple agendas" [p.1057])
5. effective communication
6. communal reflection (in addition to personal reflection) (pp. 1056–1057)

Additionally, differing from traditional sequential research strategies, the design phases may occur in recurrent order (Hadorn et al. 2008).

In the beginning, no matter what kind of project you are developing, I think the most important issue to pay attention to is time. Because of the complexity of designing a transdisciplinary research project, it is important to devote plenty of time to the percolation of ideas, preliminary research/immersion into the literature, collaborative planning (when appropriate), and the development of a research strategy. Nurturing the development of ideas (and tenets of collaboration when appropriate) is vital and should not be overlooked or rushed through.

Researchable Topics

A colleague once told me that she didn't see the point in doing research unless you could study the most important thing there is to study. While I do not agree with that, as I think there are innumerable opportunities to engage in worthwhile research projects and we do not need to make a hierarchy of importance, I do understand her point. By applying a transdisciplinary approach to research we are able to research a host of topics that would otherwise be out of reach, and we are able to address topics more holistically or comprehensively then would otherwise be possible. This opens up a vast range of possible research topics that may otherwise be beyond our disciplinary visions and capabilities.

Transdisciplinary approaches are generally used for issue- or problem-centered research topics. Moreover, ideally, there is a moral, ethical or social imperative driving the research. Topics are selected to fulfill a need in the real world—to build knowledge that is needed, is useful, and has the potential to propel social change. Transdisciplinarity allows us to research large, complex, and "significant" problems. Transdisciplinarity provides an approach for conducting *research that matters*. Some questions to consider as you select a research topic include:

- Is this a significant issue or problem in the real world?
- Is knowledge about this topic needed?
- Is there a moral or ethical imperative for researching this topic?
- Will knowledge about this topic be useful?
- Is there potential for social change?

Researchers may select topics in a variety of ways including their awareness of a pressing need/problem/issue in the community or society at large, a funding opportunity or invitation to collaborate on a project, or a long-term interest in a topic of some social significance. Transdisciplinary research topics may also be organized around a "site." This is a conceptual space where disciplines assemble (Krimsky 2000) and is likely transdisciplinary by nature. Krimsky defines this concept as follows:

> 1. a space such as an inner-city community or factory; 2. a community, such as gypsies, with shared experience; 3. a conceptual site such as drug abuse, which is specific but extends over the physical environment and many other forms of human experience; and 4. a discursive site such as debates over race or native title/land rights, in which different groups are in conflict over the interpretation of certain issues…. The site is a space in which or about which disciplines gather and proceed to engage in analysis from a variety of perspectives. From the locus of the site, we get the definition of the issues raised and the creation of team goals and objectives. (2000, 232)

Multiple "sites" may also overlap, creating the ultimate locus of the research topic.

Research Purpose and Questions

Once a general topic has been selected it is important to determine a specific research purpose or set of purposes and then to develop research questions aimed at addressing the purpose. While this is always the case in social research the process may be more complicated and time-consuming in transdisciplinary research given the complexity of the topic that may be under investigation and the need for immersion in other literatures and/or collaboration with other researchers, practitioners or community members. Fairly extensive learning or training may be needed just to form appropriate guiding questions.

The use of a transdisciplinary approach allows the asking of many new research questions that would not otherwise be possible. Identifying and structuring research questions may be particularly challenging in transdisciplinary research because of the scope and complexity of the research topic studied (Pohl et al. 2007). Transdisciplinarity does not reduce this complexity, as disciplinary applied research may, but rather embraces and goes after the real-world complexity of the issue or problem as much as possible (Pohl et al. 2007). Klein notes that a "multi-dimensional framework of questions is a key methodological tool" (2000, 8) in transdisciplinary research.

Pohl and Hadorn (2007) suggest that transdisciplinarity can address three kinds of questions, each linked with three different kinds of knowledge. The question types are:

1. Questions about the genesis and possible further development of a problem, and about interpretations of the problem in the life-world (this set of questions creates "systems knowledge")

2. Questions related to determining and explaining the need for change, desired goals and better practices (this set of questions produces "target knowledge")

3. Questions about technical, social, legal, cultural and other possible means of acting that aim to transform existing practices and introduce desired ones (this set of questions produces "transformation knowledge") (2007, 36)

Further, they acknowledge "interdependencies between the three forms of knowledge" (p. 38), and thus projects may combine these kinds of questions and knowledge outcomes.

When working collaboratively, as is often the case in transdisciplinary projects, the research questions must be agreed on. Moreover, when the research is community-based (that is, serving the needs of the community you are working with) then "the legitimacy of the research questions is also dependent on the agreement or consensus of the community" (Greckhamer et al. 2008, 318). Research questions in these projects should be developed in a highly collaborative context. In any kind of research partnership, whether researcher(s) and community partners, or a team of researchers, addressing the questions should ultimately be mutually beneficial. Pohl (2005) suggests that the process should be one of "mutual learning" (p. 1161). Since transdisciplinarity promotes forward-thinking, research should advance prior research or fill a gap in our knowledge. Greckhamer and colleagues write: "For a community of inquiry, acceptable research questions are those that continue the work of previous scholars, contributing to the existing literature, and/or have significance within the terrain of knowledge over which the community has, or claims, jurisdiction" (2008, 318).

Here are some questions to consider as you develop your research purpose and questions:

- What kind of knowledge is being sought?
- How can questions be formulated in order to get at the desired knowledge?
- How can this research extend current knowledge on the topic?
- Will this research fill a gap in our knowledge about the topic?
- Have relevant stakeholders/partners (e.g., researchers, community members) agreed on the research questions?
- Will answering the research questions be mutually beneficial to relevant stakeholders/partners?

Transdisciplinary Literature Review

In any research project the purpose of a literature review is to figure out what research has already been conducted on your topic which can assist you in a range of ways including determining the scope of your project, defining key terms, and eventually interpreting data. A literature review consists of locating, summarizing and synthesizing the current (and landmark) research on your topic. This process is much more complicated in a transdisciplinary research project because you are seeking literature in multiple relevant fields. Researchers must immerse themselves in those literatures, learning their language, and seeking the expertise of others as needed. As literature may be pulled from numerous disciplines the process of taking an "inventory" of the relevant literature alone can be a long process, and ample time must be given to building this framework (Darbellay 2008). Darbellay suggests taking inventories of what is just beyond the scope of each relevant discipline and determining where synergies can be found or forged. Synthesizing the literature is also more complex than in a disciplinary literature review. As Miller suggested back in 1982, transdisciplinarity requires the creation of holistic conceptual frameworks that transcend disciplinarity, which I suggest literature can help us build. The process of conducting a transdisciplinary literature review may require the following steps:

1. determining relevant disciplinary bodies of knowledge,

2. locating and summarizing relevant literature (current and landmark studies) from each discipline,

3. determining what is just beyond the scope of each discipline ,

4. locating existing synergies between different disciplinary resources,

5. locating and creating possible/new synergies between different disciplinary resources, and

6. synthesizing the literature in order to build a framework.

It is important to note that the preceding process may involve extensive negotiations between differently positioned research partners.

Researchers may be working with studies conducted from different paradigmatic viewpoints and may be using very different conceptual frameworks. Using the literature to define key terms is one of the most important design processes in a transdisciplinary project. This can be a challenging process because many different disciplinary perspectives may come into the mix. Additionally, culturally sensitive definitions must be sought (as relevant to the project). So, for example, in a community-based research project, definitions of key terms and concepts must be determined in a collaborative context in which community partners and very likely research participants (or community members) are involved. Terms must be relevant to the communities the research serves—to community understandings of relevant concepts. This is even more challenging in trans-cultural or transnational research where various cultural perspectives are also brought to bear on the process.

Here an excellent example comes from a transdisciplinary endeavor called "The Household, Gender, and Age Project." This ten-year cross-cultural project was highly complex, focusing on the effects of macro events on the family unit and women in eight developing countries. The genesis of the project occurred when three scholars from different parts of the world (Africa, Europe and North America) participated in a program advisory committee, organized by the United Nations University, aimed at dealing with major contemporary challenges such as development. Through their participation the researchers came to the realization that the committee was "gender-blind" and working from the assumption that the labor force was male (Boulding 1991, xi). Put simply, women weren't being properly included. Elise Boulding writes:

> Wenche Barth Eide of Norway, Frede Chale of Kenya, and I wondered how a more differentiated perception of women and men as agents of change with different but overlapping roles, responsibilities, and contributions could be inserted into development models. We thought in terms of relating macro-phenomenon to the micro-realities of daily life. We sought a perspective that could make women visible.... The answer was the household. Here, in all its cultural diversity, is the primary living unit of human beings, where the species is reproduced and nurtured, the base from which individuals participate in the whole range of tasks that shape and change a community and a society. Looking at people in households means seeing each member as an individual, a source of reproduction and production, a resistance to change and of change. It means seeing men and women, children and old people in relation to their community as well as in relation to each other. (Boulding 1991, xi)

Clearly, from the outset this project was problem-driven. With the problem of including women in long-term development research in the developing world at the center of all research efforts, from initial planning to representing the findings, the researchers were guided by the principles of transdisciplinarity. The research team aimed to impact policy so that women's situations would be properly included in policy planning (Boulding 1991) by targeting national and international decision-makers who may not know women's needs in different regions (Masini 1991).

This ten-year project that involved studies conducted across the developing world cannot be replicated here. However, the story of how the team developed the project and each sub-study illustrates how a large and diverse research team can work together in order to build an appropriate conceptual structure. Perhaps more than anything, this multi-faceted project illustrates the challenges of transnational research, particularly incorporating different cultural and disciplinary perspectives into the project, but simultaneously how a transdisciplinary approach can make this possible. It took the team one year just to develop an appropriate transdisciplinary approach (showing the significance of the planning stage). The approach involved historical, sociological, demographic, ethnological, statistical and mathematical analysis and used multi-method and mixed method designs that included a life-course approach (Masini 2000).

One of the main challenges during the first year was developing a transdisciplinary definition of "the household" that works in the eight different cultural contexts. Here both disciplinary and cultural issues emerge. With respect to the former, the researchers worked together and came to view the term

> from an economic point of view in terms of income; from a sociological point of view in terms of numbers of members of the household; from a psychological perspective in terms of interrelations within the family; from a historical point of view in terms of changes in the household; and from an anthropological point of view in terms of co-residence. (Masini 2000, 122)

It was equally important to consider how cultural understandings of "the household" differ across contexts. Therefore, in addition to considering the conventional Western notion of the household (co-residence) the team also included other cultural understandings of the household such as kinship and obligations of non-resident "household" members to resident members (such as financial or childcare obligations) (Masini 1991).

Balancing different bodies of literature as well as the perspectives of the different players involved can be taxing but when done with care can result in the creation of appropriate and highly effective concepts that allow researchers to access the dimensions of social life they are after.

Although the team worked together in order to build the conceptual structure of the project they also deemed it important to acknowledge and include the insider cultural knowledge of the individual researchers as well as their disciplinary and practical skill sets. Therefore, the larger research team ultimately created eight different projects each conducted in a different country and led by a different principle investigator or investigators from that country. These studies all stand on their own but are also a part of this larger cross-cultural, longitudinal project.

For each study the research team investigated how macro events impact the household, particularly women. Changes and issues considered included: migration to those countries, economic changes, technological changes, ecological changes, rates of labor force participation, family planning (including fertility and sexuality), education, socioeconomic conditions, "domestic power structures" and how psychosociological levels of experience are impacted by macro changes. Each of the eight research projects focused on a macro event or macro events relevant to the particular community under investigation. For example, the Kenya research project focused on changes in labor at tea and coffee plantations that produce the main crops and exports of the agricultural country (Masini 1991). The focal point of that sub-study was "on the role of the household as a unit integrated into the contemporary plantation economy" (Masini 1991, 14).

For each study the research team in that location also determined the appropriate methodological strategy. So the larger overarching project included many different research design strategies. In the case of the Kenya study a mixed method strategy was employed. The team used multiple quantitative questionnaires as well as fieldwork that included systematic observations and qualitative interviews. Following the methodological principles of good quantitative questionnaire construction, the team pretested and revised the questionnaires in order to ensure that they would access the data they were after in a way that was understandable to their research participants. The data collection occurred at three tea and coffee plantations, each of which was over 60 years old (enabling a historical perspective, or social change perspective, to emerge). The researchers engaged in many negotiations with the management of the plantations who acted as "gatekeepers" in order to carry out this research. In total 600 participants were interviewed, 400 women and 200 men, in sessions lasting two to three hours. While some were given permission to be interviewed during work time due to the perceived importance of the research, other participants lost up to a day's wages. (For a discussion of the research findings see Agadala 1991.)

"The Household, Gender, and Age Project" developed in order to address a pressing transnational social problem. With that in mind, a truly diverse group of researchers were able to organize around the problem at hand and bring in their diverse disciplinary, practical and cultural knowledge in order to serve the research project. The success of this project is largely a result of the willingness of the team to spend ample time developing a conceptual structure for the research that worked across contexts while also allowing specific cultural concerns to take center stage, and methodologies to be developed accordingly.

The Division of Labor

In collaborative or team research it is important to clearly define tasks, roles, expectations and responsibilities as a part of the planning process (if you are conducting research alone and the transdisciplinarity of the project is based on the resources you are using and framework you are building, you may skip this section). This process is twofold: one dimension includes determining the division of labor, and the other dimension includes creating the context of transdisciplinary collaboration.

In terms of determining the division of labor, the process of defining roles and expectations should not be rushed through as it is vital that team members build a solid foundation from which to work. During this process team members should clearly define the steps that will be taken (and build time for review, repetition and revision as necessary) in relation to their goals (which should also be determined collaboratively). It is important to decide individuals' roles and responsibilities. In short, the team must answer the questions:

- What will be done?
- Who will do what and by when?
- How will team members assist each other?

Although the effort will be collaborative, it is also important to determine the leadership structure for the project. Oftentimes it is helpful to have someone or some group who is responsible for keeping things on course. Further, even in collaborative research some team members may be more invested in the project for any number of reasons. This must be factored into the division of labor and leadership structure as appropriate. When planning the leadership structure individual or disciplinary "power" can come into play, even if unintentionally. Open communication and reflexivity can help alleviate the unintended replication of dominant relations of power (between researchers and their community partners; between the natural and social sciences; between the natural sciences and humanities or arts; and so forth).

Finally, when determining each member's role in the process it is important to come to an understanding about the research outcomes.

- What are the expected outcomes?
- How will the research findings be reported and disseminated?
- Will there be multiple outcomes?

- What will be co-authored, and how will that transpire?
- What will be single authored, and how will that occur?
- How will the team work be identified in any single or co-authored work?
- What data will be "communal" and what "belongs" to certain team members, and why?

This planning process is not only a means of determining the division of labor but also creating a productive space in which team members can become acclimated to each other and each other's disciplinary perspective (or other experiential expertise) and can develop some common understandings of how the process will unfold. In this regard, this process can help sensitize research partners to their own perspectives so that they are more able to challenge their own assumptions and thus fully engage with the possibilities of transdisciplinary vision. Depending on the particular project individuals involved in this process may include any combination of researchers, practitioners, members of community-based organizations, and research participants. It is critical that during this planning phase team members, who will be coming to the project with different perspectives and experiences, find ways to bridge differences in "methods, work styles, and epistemologies" (Klein 2004, 520). This period, therefore, provides an opportunity for team-building, rapport-building, and cross-disciplinary learning in a variety of ways. Language and communication are vital in team work and, therefore, since research partners come to the process speaking different disciplinary languages, it is important to spend time developing common understandings, defining key concepts, and building effective approaches to communication. In funded research ample time for planning and team-building should be built into the grant structure. Moreover, if some participants work at community-based organizations or are lay members of the community involved in the research, their ability (time/financial) to participate in this stage of the process should be considered in advance.

Any necessary recruiting (for research partners or participants) and training should also be planned during this stage. For example, researchers may have to be taught the tenets of quantitative or qualitative approaches to research which may differ from their past experience. For instance, they may need to learn how to conduct unstructured interviews or how to moderate focus group interviews. Researchers may have to learn how to use computer-driven data analysis packages that they are unfamiliar with, or they may have to learn the workings of a particular community-based organization, or perhaps the process of art-making in some particular genre or style, or any other number of skills/practices with which they are unfamiliar. Issues of recruiting and training are discussed further in the next chapter on community-based research.

Research Design: Data Collection

Transdisciplinary research is characterized as a problem-centered approach to research. Therefore, the methods (tools used to gather data) are always selected in relation to the specific problem or issue at hand. Methods are selected for their utility in eliciting or generating appropriate data (Hesse-Biber & Leavy 2011). There are no methods that are inherently transdisciplinary—transdisciplinarity is an *approach* to research. Any methods or methods combinations may be employed, including traditional disciplinary methods such as case studies, interviews, surveys, experiments, ethnography, document analysis, historical comparative research, focus groups, oral histories and life stories; hybrid methods (which may mix the tenets of the qualitative and quantitative paradigms); and, other cross-disciplinary methods innovations (such as arts-based research practices). Transdisciplinary approaches to research may result in methodological innovations (and often do) that go beyond traditional mixed-methods designs and result in the creation of new research strategies. To summarize, transdisciplinary projects may use any number of research methods and methods designs in service of addressing the issue or problem at hand, including:

- traditional qualitative or quantitative methods
- hybrid methods
- cross-disciplinary methods
- multi-methods
- mixed methods

It is important to note that while I suggest traditional disciplinary methods may be employed in transdisciplinary research, they cease to be "disciplinary" when applied through a transdisciplinary approach. In other words, while surveys or interviews, for example, are used in disciplinary research projects, when the perspective and approach is transdisciplinary, the same method (surveys or interviews) is being employed in a very different way. Nicolescu writes: "The transdisciplinary method does not replace the methodology of each discipline, which remains as it is. Instead the transdisciplinary method enriches each of these disciplines by bringing them new and indispensable insights, which cannot be produced by disciplinary methods" (2002, 122).

There is wide acknowledgement within the research community that methodological innovation abounds (for example see Hesse-Biber & Leavy 2006, 2008; Leavy 2009; Van Manen 2001). For instance, Van Manen writes: "Researchers now employ methods and approaches that have moved far beyond traditional discipline-based methodologies and methods" (2001, 851). Transdisciplinary concerns have provided the push for many methodological innovations, and transdisciplinarity has simultaneously created the context in which such innovations can emerge.

I now move into a brief review of mixed method and multi-method designs as well as hybrid research designs, including examples of some commonly used methods innovations.

Mixed Methods or Multi-Methods

Transdisciplinary projects typically require the use of more than one method (although this is a norm, it is by no means a requirement). Therefore, many transdisciplinary projects follow mixed methods or multi-method designs which involve the use of more than one data collection method. Transdisciplinary projects often require the use of multiple methods because the problem or issue addressed is complex and multi-faceted. Transdisciplinarity does not reduce this complexity but enables us to better see and investigate it. Additionally, triangulation is often practiced in order to build validity and trustworthiness into the findings (Connor, Treloar & Higginbotham 2001).

Mixed methods designs are those which use methods from at least two different paradigms (typically, a qualitative and quantitative method). So, for example, mixed methods designs may include the use of surveys and in-depth interviews, or statistical analysis and qualitative document analysis, or many other combinations. These approaches involve the mixing of methodological tools that are based on different epistemological and ontological assumptions. These design formats are particularly common in transdisciplinary projects when researchers from different disciplines collaborate (such as the natural and social sciences). Sometimes three or more methods are used in a triangulated model.

For example, "The Household, Gender, and Age Project" reviewed earlier in this chapter is an example of mixed methods research. Not only did the overarching project include a variety of methodological strategies from across research paradigms, smaller studies within the project relied on mixed methods designs. For instance, the Kenyan tea and coffee plantation study noted employed both quantitative questionnaires and qualitative interviews.

Multi-method designs also involve the use of at least two methods but do not involve the mixing of paradigmatic viewpoints. So, a multi-method project may involve the use of two or more qualitative methods (such as ethnography and in-depth interviews) or two or more quantitative methods (such as surveys and statistical analysis of census data). These projects are typically carried out by individual researchers or researchers who share similar disciplinary backgrounds (or come from similar paradigmatic backgrounds within different disciplines), although this is not always the case and may simply result from the topic and questions driving the research.

For example, the large-scale study conducted on the health status of Hungarian populations reviewed earlier involved researchers from many different disciplines and relied on a six part methodology that included multiple survey protocols and the analysis of statistical data (Piko & Kopp 2008). One could envision adding qualitative methods to that study (such as interviews, focus groups or daily diary research) and transforming the multi-method study into a mixed methods study.

Of course, in transdisciplinary research projects researchers are often required to work outside of their typical methods "comfort zone" (see Hesse-Biber & Leavy 2006, 2008 for a discussion of methods "comfort zones") so these generalizations refer to norms and not dictates. Often researchers will be willing and able to learn new viewpoints, methods and approaches, and some research grants and design strategies account for this needed training. However, equally true, disciplinarity (and all the training and expertise that comes with it) can be a big asset in many transdisciplinary projects and therefore may require researchers to practice what they already know, but in new ways or new contexts.

In their best form, mixed method and multi-method designs offer holistic approaches to research where each component of the research speaks to the other components (Hesse-Biber & Leavy 2011; Hesse-Biber 2011). In other words, in their best execution, the use of multiple methods is not simply additive (more methods, more data), but rather, the use of each method informs the use of the other methods (Hesse-Biber & Leavy 2011; Hesse-Biber 2011). Although this is the ideal form of mixed methods research, I suggest that the potential of mixed methods research is rarely reached. Most often the methods are used in a series of linear steps where one method is privileged over the other (one paradigm is privileged over the other). Generally speaking, quantitative data is privileged with qualitative data serving in a secondary capacity, often as an add-on and source for quotes in published research reports, but with little bearing on how the research was conducted and what was found. I suggest that transdisciplinarity, which requires integrated, holistic and synergistic approaches to research can go well beyond the promises of mixed method designs, and can help promote the kinds of holistic approaches to mixed methods research that are held as the ideal. In other words, *a transdisciplinary perspective can strengthen mixed methods research practice.*

There are also specific methodological strategies that can be used as vehicles for mixing methods in transdisciplinary research. I offer a couple of examples: "social network analysis" and "extended case method."

Social Network Analysis and Extended Case Method

"Social network analysis" and "extended case method" are two methodological innovations for studying transdisciplinary topics such as public policy. *Social network analysis* is useful for examining how public policy shapes society (or aspects of society) because, differing from traditional approaches which may only gather data on either the micro or macro level, social network analysis can be used to examine policy from multiple levels (Wedel, Shore, Feldman & Lathrop 2005). Wedel and colleagues elaborate on this as follows: "By linking actors, network analysis can show how the local or regional level is connected with the national level or the local, regional, or national level with the international" (2005, 40). Social network analysis is a multi-method research strategy (that may involve ethnography, interviews, document analysis and other methods) employed in transdisciplinary studies in order to study, for example, transnational policy processes (Wedel et al. 2005). Social network analysis is not only a method but also "an orienting idea" (Scott 1991, 37) that can be particularly useful for studying transnational policy processes (Wedel et al. 2005) which is a transdisciplinary domain of inquiry. Wedel and colleagues point to the need for a transdisciplinary approach to public policy research: "The value of a theoretical and methodological framework that can both dissect and connect levels (such as local and global) and spheres (such as state and private) is difficult to overstate in a multi-layered and rapidly changing world" (2005, 41). Similarly, the "extended case method" is also used to make micro-macro and local-global links (Wedel et al. 2005). Wedel writes: "Although actors included in a particular 'case' sometimes are located in different sites, they always are connected by the policy process and/or by actual social networks" (2005, 41). This approach is increasingly valuable in a globalized world in which people impacted by particular policies may be geographically, culturally, technologically and/or economically scattered.

Hybrid Research Designs

Sometimes transdisciplinary efforts result in the development of hybrid methodological strategies (see Leavy 2008; Porteous et al. 2001). In this regard Klein and colleagues write: "Existing and new approaches are combined in a collaborative effort to create new spaces and cultures of mutuality" (2004, 44).

Qualitative Case-Control and Contrasting Groups Framework

Porteous, Higginbotham, Freeman and Connor (2001) suggest two "hybrid study designs" that are frequently used in transdisciplinary research: "qualitative case-control design" and the "contrasting groups framework." These two designs may be particularly useful for "exploring non-linear relationships" (Porteous et al. 2001, 337). These approaches combine the strengths of both quantitative and qualitative approaches (Porteous et al. 2001), creating hybrid techniques that go beyond traditional mixed methods. Qualitative case-control expands on the possibilities of case studies. Poretous and colleagues note the primary principle of case-control (in health studies) as follows:

> Subjects may be categorized as cases or controls using a range of criteria such as disease status (presence or absence of heart disease), health behavior (smoking or non-smoking, Pap smear or no Pap smear), or psychological profile (depressed, not depressed). The important thing is that the cases, those having the outcome of interest, can be clearly distinguished from those that do not (controls). A range of qualitative techniques... are then employed to fully explore the sociocultural, environmental, and other factors relevant to both groups. (Porteous et al. 2001, 311)

The research team explains "contrasting groups framework" as follows:

> In the contrasting groups design, subjects in a survey are first assigned a score according to some agreed performance criteria and then rank ordered according to that score, from greatest to least. The researcher then selects subjects from the top and bottom of the rankings. In doing so, two contrasting groups are created that will become the focus for intensive qualitative follow up. The criteria on which subjects are ranked can be derived from previous work in the area or *de novo* by the researcher. There are no strict rules for how to define the contrasting groups. (Porteous et al. 2001, 321)

Again, these are just examples of hybrid research designs with many other possibilities. Like with other forms of mixing methods, in transdisciplinary projects these designs require holistic and integrated approaches.

Photovoice

There are also hybrid research methods that emerge out of the tenets and practices of other methods combinations (technological progress may fuel the development of these techniques as well). One such innovation frequently used in transdisciplinary research is "photovoice." *Photovoice* is a commonly used method in a variety of transdisciplinary efforts that maintain a social action orientation. This participatory method involves having participants take photographs to document their experiences, situations or environments and can be used in many different research genres. Examples of the kinds of projects in which photovoice is used range from arts-based approaches to social topics, such as poverty or development, to community-based research in health and other topics. Holm (2008) notes that photovoice has become particularly popular in public health research. In community-based research, a genre in which the use of photovoice is expanding greatly, participants take photographs which they can use to advocate for community improvement (Berg 2007; Holm 2008). In these contexts photovoice may be used as a part of public policy work. One can envision photovoice being used with a social network analysis framework, for example. I suggest that photovoice combines the tenets of social action research, participatory research, and arts-based research and is useful in a variety of transdisciplinary research contexts. Wang (2005, www.photovoice.com/method/index.html) suggests the following model when designing a study that employs photovoice:

> Conceptualizing the problem; defining broader goals and objectives; recruiting policymakers as the audience for photovoice findings; training the trainers; conducting photovoice training; devising the initial theme/s for taking pictures; taking pictures; facilitating group discussion; critical reflection and dialogue; selecting photographs for discussion; contextualizing and storytelling; codifying issues, themes, and theories; documenting the stories; conducting the formative evaluation; reaching policymakers, donors, media, researchers, and others who may be mobilized to create change. (as quoted in Holm 2008, 330)

Researchers from any discipline can be trained to use this method, and one can imagine it being employed in a great range of transdisciplinary contexts in service of many different kinds of research objectives.

Research Design: Analysis, Interpretation and Representation

Issues of analysis, interpretation and representation are reflected on further in chapter 6 during the discussion of evaluation strategies; however, at this point I review some of the general issues and practices that emerge frequently in the literature.

Analysis and Interpretation

Data analysis strategies will vary depending on the methods employed in the study, and techniques should be selected accordingly. Whether the study uses quantitative, qualitative or mixed methods, computer-assisted analysis programs are available and may be useful. When a transdisciplinary project is collaborative, involving multiple stakeholders, a collaborative analysis strategy should be employed. Transdisciplinary research is often a group undertaking involving research teams or individual researchers working with other research partners (such as practitioners, community organizations, and/or participants). In these circumstances different research partners may come to the analysis process with different skills and perspectives. This should be accounted for when determining an analysis protocol. Examples of strategies include:

cross-checking preliminary findings (which can be repeated in cycles) (Flinterman et al. 2001), also referred to as "analysis cycles" (Tenni, Smith & Boucher 2003);[3] having one party take responsibility for analysis/coding and then circulating the analyzed data to the other research partners for comment; and continuous feedback loops and re-checking assumptions (Flinterman et al. 2001). Following any of these strategies may result in the building of "intersubjectivity," which builds validity and trustworthiness into the data. In a transdisciplinary project achieving "intersubjectivity" is particularly meaningful because it implies that the various disciplinary perspectives came together to move beyond their individual disciplinary capabilities. In short, intersubjectivity is a major achievement in transdisciplinary research.

Earlier in this chapter we saw the building of intersubjectivity in "The Household, Gender, and Age Project" in which researchers spent a year coming to shared definitions of key concepts, such as the household, that would work across highly diverse cultural contexts. In the following chapter on community-based research we will again see intersubjectivity at work in Lukehart's recounting of a large-scale project on community development and segregation in Chicago. The large research partnership of twelve academics and many professional, activist and lay participants was broken down into smaller teams, each designated a study within the larger project (much like "The Household, Gender, and Age Project"). At multiple points the smaller research groups returned to the larger group to discuss strategies and findings. By disavowing individual "authority" and engaging in feedback loops, the team was able to build intersubjectivity into the eventual findings (which importantly were used to impact local public policies).

By researchers engaging in analysis loops and related strategies, rigor may be achieved and later evidenced. *Rigor* is often held as a primary evaluative standard in social research. Nicolescu (2002) posits that the three characteristics of a transdisciplinary perspective are rigor, opening, and tolerance. Engaging in cycles of analysis and feedback in some form can promote these dimensions of transdisciplinarity. Nicolescu (2002) writes:

> Rigor is… the result of [a] perpetual search continually nourished by new knowledge and new experiences. The rigor of transdisciplinarity is of the same nature as scientific rigor but the languages are different. One can even assert that the rigor of transdisciplinarity is a deepening of scientific rigor to the extent that it takes into account not only things,

but also beings and their relation to other beings and things. Taking account of all of the givens present in a particular situation is a characteristic of this rigor. It is only in this way that rigor is truly a safeguard against all possible wrong turns. Opening brings an acceptance of the unknown, the unexpected and the unpredictable. (p. 120)

Truly collaborative analysis processes will involve the questioning and challenging of assumptions. This can be a difficult process. One of the hurdles researchers working collaboratively may experience is letting go of sole ownership of the analysis process. Frisch (1990) coined the term "sharing authority" which denotes sharing ownership in the meaning-making process. As will be reviewed in chapter 6, fully engaging with an iterative process or "responsive methodology" is another way of achieving rigor and building trustworthiness into the data. So, too, researchers must consider carefully the extent to which their methodology has effectively addressed their research questions. Also discussed in chapter 6 are a range of other benchmarks, such as "vigor," which may be a goal in arts-based research, for example.

To summarize, strategies of analysis may include:

- computer-assisted analysis programs
- crosschecking preliminary findings
- analysis cycles
- one party initially analyzes the data which has been circulated to other research partners and/or differently positioned stakeholders
- continuous feedback loops and rechecking assumptions (as a part of an iterative or "responsive" approach)
- "sharing authority"

A transdisciplinary approach to data interpretation, whether in collaborative or individual research, involves the use of multiple bodies of literature. Earlier immersion in transdisciplinary literature (used during research design) also comes to bear in the interpretation process. Literature from relevant (meaning useful) fields can be used to make sense out of the data. During this process, theories on the macro level might be used to help make sense of micro level data and vice versa.

As different disciplinary viewpoints are being brought in to help make sense out of the data, it is important to remain reflexive about one's own disciplinary perspective. Reflexivity is necessary in order to be able to "see" the big picture from multiple vantage points. In a collaborative project it is important to be open to differing interpretations. While respect and openness are necessary, productive debate and negotiation may be assets as well—not debate for the sake of being "right" but as a means of working out alternative interpretations and stretching one's vision. A robust interpretive process will strengthen the research findings.

To summarize, strategies of interpretation generally include:

- using literature to make sense out of the data
- applying theory to the data
- collaboration, discussion and negotiation with research partners and/or differently positioned stakeholders

During the interpretive process it is important to remain reflexive about how your disciplinary perspective comes to bear on your understandings and assumptions.

Representation and Dissemination

Transdisciplinary research is intended to be useful—to address some real-world issue or problem. Therefore, it is vital to circumvent the typical academic publishing routine, where research is published only in highly specialized journals with very limited audiences. Rather, transdisciplinary research findings should be represented in accessible formats and disseminated in appropriate contexts and communities. While it *is* important to publish academic journal articles so that the research community can draw on previous research, it is unlikely that a traditional academic article would be the only outcome warranted.

First and foremost transdisciplinary research should reach diverse and public audiences (in addition to relevant audiences within the research community). When engaging in a transdisciplinary project there is an ethical obligation to ensure that the groups we aim to serve have access to the research findings. Making research accessible to nonacademic audiences requires 1) new representational forms and 2) new venues for dissemination.[4]

Making the research findings useful beyond the academy, while a subject that receives a fair amount of discussion at a theoretical level, is an objective that is often under-realized in disciplinary and interdisciplinary research practice. Transdisciplinary researchers, however, have made enormous strides in this regard, creating a host of new ways to represent and disseminate research findings. Representational forms beyond traditional academic prose (research articles) may include (but are not limited to):

- newspapers articles (such as op-ed articles)
- pamphlets
- newsletters and other informational booklets
- bulletin board postings
- radio broadcasts
- public lectures (in community-based organizations and other community locations)
- conference presentations (which may follow traditional or innovative formats)
- books (which may be trade non-fiction or fiction as well as academic books)
- art installations/displays
- photographic installations/displays
- dramatic, musical, dance or spoken word performances
- written or read poetry
- fictionalized writing in short or long formats
- documentary films
- websites or video diaries

For example, in the following chapter on community-based research I review two projects that addressed cancer disparities in black Floridian populations. In order to best serve the relevant communities and advance future research, the findings were represented in multiple forms, including culturally and literacy sensitive informational pamphlets, local news and traditional academic articles.

The different formats for representation also signal the different venues (beyond academic journals) in which research findings may circulate. For example:

- local newspapers
- local radio broadcasts
- community centers
- art galleries
- local performance centers
- churches and other community spaces

- the Internet
- poetry and literary magazines
- other venues

Returning to the Florida cancer study example, the researchers distributed the findings in local newspapers, community spaces (barber shops) and other venues.

The Internet has created a host of "publishing" possibilities that did not formerly exist. For example, online journals and other online forums allow for the relatively inexpensive publishing of photographic and other visual materials (made even easier with the proliferation of digital cameras). Likewise, sound and audiovisual files are also easily published online. In this regard, *YouTube, Facebook,* and other free (or low-cost) websites make the sharing of these kinds of materials far simpler than ever before, and more accessible to wider audiences.

These new or "alternative" forms of representation and avenues for dissemination should be selected for their fit with the particular project objectives. As you determine appropriate representational forms and venues, consider the following questions:

- Who are you trying to reach?
- What "languages" are going to be most understandable, informative and helpful to those populations you are trying to reach?
- What forms will make the research findings come to life? What are you trying to accomplish (bridging differences, breaking stereotypes, building critical consciousness, education, empowerment, and so on)?
- What forms will be most able to achieve those goals? (Of course practical issues such as time, funding, access to needed resources, and so forth also come into the process, as elaborated in chapter 6).

Often transdisciplinary research will result in more than one outcome. When there are multiple outcomes, they may take different representational forms (Austin et al. 2008). Typically researchers do publish research articles out of their findings (which in team research may result in multiple articles with different disciplinary audiences in mind). However, researchers often use the other formats noted in addition to academic articles, allowing them to work and advance within the traditional academic career trajectory while also making their findings more accessible to, and useful for, broader audiences.

Chapter Four

Community-Based Research Practices
Designing Problem-Centered Collaborations

The candle is not there to illuminate itself.
—Nowab Jan-Fishan Khan, nineteenth century

Community-based research (CBR) involves collaborative partnerships between the research/academic community and community members. CBR is an attempt for researchers to actively involve the communities that they claim to serve through the research process. Researchers will often partner with established community-based organizations (CBOs) (although this is not always the case).

It is important to note from the outset that a great deal of community-based research occurs in order to teach undergraduate students. For example, professors and service learning professionals may develop community-based research projects for their classes. While ideally these projects also serve the needs of the relevant communities, this is not always the case as these projects are typically structured around the academic calendar and the needs of individual professors and their students. This is a complicated subject and one that I am not going to take up in this chapter. As my interest in community-based research is in the context of exploring transdisciplinarity, I focus exclusively on research conducted by researchers (with their community partners) for the sake of their own research and community betterment.

The history of CBR is intertwined with the history of social action research and participatory research (community-based participatory research, CBPR, is considered one approach to CBR; however, given the relatively brief treatment of CBR in this book I employ the more general term CBR). CBR developed because universities had been viewed by many as detached and unresponsive to the needs of the community (Strand, Marullo, Cutforth, Stoecker & Donohue 2003). In this vein, CBR is a strategy for placing the research community/academy within real-world contexts, and not outside of them. Therefore, there is a natural synergy between CBR and transdisciplinarity.

Community-based research, in its ideal form, is a holistic, synergistic, and highly collaborative approach to research. Whether an individual researcher is embarking on a CBR project with community partners, or whether a team of multi-disciplinary researchers is engaging in a CBR project, CBR is a necessarily collaborative approach to research. CBR requires researchers to share authority over the knowledge-building process. Community-based research projects share a commitment to social action, social change and social justice (Strand 2003).

Community-based research developed in multi- and interdisciplinary research contexts, and is not the methodological property of any one discipline. I suggest that in its best form CBR is necessarily a transdisciplinary modality of research. Although at its best CBR is transdisciplinary, the fact is that for a host of practical and other reasons most CBR projects are not transdisciplinary. CBR is not inherently transdisciplinary, but rather a transdisciplinary approach may be applied to a CBR study. The core principles and design issues reviewed in this chapter and summarized later in table 4.1 represent the criteria for a CBR project to be deemed transdisciplinary. In order to maximize the benefits of CBR, researchers developing projects need to cultivate transdisciplinary perspectives and attend to the challenges that are part and parcel of such an endeavor. One research genre in which this has been occurring is health research.

Over the past few decades transdisciplinary approaches to community-based research have flourished in health studies. There are several factors that likely impact this trend. To begin with, the kind of health problems that have grown in recent decades (cancer, diabetes, HIV/AIDS, obesity) can be prevented or better treated with education, behavioral changes and/or early intervention. Secondly, we have a lot of new information about the benefits of holistic approaches to health. In this regard, in 1984 the World Health Organization defined human health "in terms of combined biological, mental and social well-being with relation to environment" (Pikot & Kopp 2008, 307). Finally, in accord with increases in multi- and inter- and transdisciplinary education, in conjunction with moves in the health community towards holistic approaches to health, several new, hybrid research fields have emerged and gained popularity.

Biomedical research, which merges medical and biological science, has grown rapidly (Flinterman et al. 2001). As biomedical research has developed, patients have simultaneously advocated for more participation in the research process (Flinterman et al. 2001). Consequently, biomedical research has trended towards transdisciplinary participatory approaches, often turning to CBR. Flinterman and colleagues note that the turn to transdisciplinary approaches to biomedical research "may result in a more structural participation of patients and more deliberate and optimal integration of their knowledge into research processes" (2001, 257).

The biopsychosocial model is another recent development in transdisciplinary approaches to health (Piko & Kopp 2008). This emerging body integrates the natural and social sciences (theories and methods). The guiding assumption in biopsychosocial models is that a patient's physical body is also deeply impacted by his or her psychosocial processes and research must get at these issues in different ways. Piko and Kopp suggest that "medicine should become an integrated scientific field, at the crossroads of the natural and social sciences, needing a transdisciplinary approach" (2008, 309).

The shift towards transdisciplinarity in health research has coincided with trends towards CBR, resulting in an increase in community-based participatory approaches to health studies. This research advances transdisciplinarity. Let's look at an in-depth example.

Health disparities across racial, ethnic and social class lines are a persistent problem in the United States, with cancer disparities now receiving considerable attention from the research community. Thinking about these disparities requires going beyond biological/medical perspectives and also paying attention to several social issues that may impact the health profile of a group or community:

- access to healthcare information and screenings
- access to quality medical care
- ways that gender, race, ethnicity, religion, sexual orientation and/or social class influence health screenings
- what makes health education effective or ineffective for different groups and why (in terms of content, form, and distribution)

There are also environmental factors that come into play such as:

- pollution
- exposures to toxic materials
- water and air quality
- food quality (such as the high price and limited availability of organics)

Therefore, this is a transdisciplinary topic by nature. In order to get at the relevant issues, research needs to connect different bodies of knowledge from the natural sciences, environmental sciences and social sciences.

The Tampa Bay Community Cancer Network (TBCCN) is a transdisciplinary organization that was forged in order to study cancer disparities in Florida and create effective health interventions in multiethnic, medically underserved communities. With funding from the National Cancer Institute the TBCCN partnered with local organizations and piloted several studies.

Meade, Menard, Luque, Martinez-Tyson and Gwede (2009) conducted two pilot studies on cancer disparities for TBCCN. Looking at the problem holistically, the team realized that the issue necessitated taking seriously recent transdisciplinary developments in embodiment theory. In this regard Meade and colleagues quote Krieger as follows: "We take it as a basic fact that we all live and act in bodies that literally embody biologically, across the life course—our societal and ecological contexts" (2005, 8, as quoted in Meade et al. 2009, 2). Therefore, the team combined the tenets of different relevant disciplines into a transdisciplinary conceptual structure larger than the sum of its parts. In this regard they applied a "socio-ecological framework" and considered the "embodiment of lifetime exposures" (2009, 2) in order to understand cancer disparities. Given the complexity of the conditions which caused disparities in health the research team needed to develop innovative approaches to the problem. The primary objective was to serve community needs, and thus the principles of community-based participatory research were used.

The research team identified two levels of needs, the first with respect to empirical research initiatives and the second with respect to health promotion programs. Therefore, each pilot study involved the development of a research initiative and an outreach component.

The first study investigated colorectal cancer, which is the third leading cause of cancer deaths among Americans, with US blacks having the highest colorectal cancer rate and mortality rate of all groups (Meade et al. 2009). Given the dangers in grouping all black people into one homogeneous category, due to possible ethnic differences with respect to food preferences and other differences, the team decided to study three ethnic subgroups of US blacks. The research team recognized that in order to garner support and participation from the community of interest it was vital to employ the principles of community-based participatory research during all phases of the research. Therefore the research team created a cultural advisory group which they used during research design, determining the scope of the project, recruitment and all the way through data interpretation. Meade and colleagues explain the methodological implications and necessity of their participatory approach as follows: "Cultural advisors proved to be a critical asset to understanding and overcoming study design and recruitment barriers. They served as ambassadors and cultural brokers who facilitated linkage to community events and cultural organizations serving the populations of interest" (2009, 4).

Based on what they learned working with their advisory group they developed a mixed methods approach to the research, demonstrating the methodological principle responsiveness as a means of staying problem-centered. The sample consisted of twenty men and women in each of the three ethnic subgroups. The mixed-method design included sequential in-depth qualitative interviews followed by quantitative questionnaires administered verbally by a trained interviewer (Meade et al. 2009).

This pilot project led to additional collaborations and concrete outcomes for the community in which the research occurred. For example, the team from TBCCN is working with a geographic information systems (GIS) expert in order to create a map of cancer screening resources in the community (Meade et al. 2009).

The second study also looked at cancer disparities in the African American male population. Specifically, the study addressed early screening for prostate cancer which is the second leading kind of cancer in this population, and again, African-American men have both a higher incidence and mortality rate than any other group (Meade et al. 2009). There is a range of complex issues that converge to create barriers to prostate cancer screening in this population. Preliminary research showed these issues include cultural definitions and performances of masculinity, distrust of the healthcare system, and fatalism regarding cancer (Meade et al. 2009). Clearly, in order to effectively address this topic in light of the issues just mentioned, bodies of literature that deal with racism, gender, race and healthcare, and the public's perception of cancer, all needed to be a part of any comprehensive approach to this problem. This project required a transdisciplinary approach.

One of the needs identified by the researchers was to create cancer awareness materials that could be easily accessed and understood by the target population. They write: "Cancer awareness materials such as brochures, booklets, and fact sheets are valuable tools used to disseminate information to the community; however, many materials are not always culturally and literacy appropriate nor easily accessible to all population groups" (Meade et al. 2009, 5).

Therefore, the researchers decided to construct a three-part study. In the first phase of the project the researchers aimed to develop customized cancer awareness materials that would be accessible and understandable to the relevant community. In order to do this the research team partnered with local barbers in order to develop the materials and a protocol for distributing them. The researchers elected to carry out the project at barber shops because they are known to attract large numbers of African-American men in the participating communities. This venue was also selected because preliminary research showed it to be deemed a "trustworthy" site within the community, with trust being previously identified as a major hurdle when conducting health research with this population. In the second phase of the research, the team developed a "lay health advisor training curriculum" in order to prepare the barbers to distribute the materials. During this phase of the research the curriculum was put into practice and the participating barbers were trained. The final phase of the research consisted of an assessment regarding the feasibility of using barbers to distribute health information and whether or not that would lead to discussions about cancer screening options with the participants' healthcare providers (Meade et al. 2009).

This pilot project has also propelled additional efforts. For example, the TBCCN is creating a "Barbershop Advisory Council" and taking steps to maintain the availability of the cancer awareness materials and "information stations in the barber shops" (Meade et al. 2009).

Like the colorectal cancer study, this project is an example of taking seriously the promises of both transdisciplinary and community-based participatory research. The research team learned about the population of interest, created a responsive research design that accounted for relevant information about the population, and included the community partners during every phase of the research. Importantly, the research team also accounted for the community's needs when determining how the research results would be disseminated (to maximize the benefits to the population of interest).

Core Principles and Research Design Issues

In order to understand the promises and perils of community-based research as a transdisciplinary undertaking it is important to first review the core principles of CBR. Of course, as is always the case, there are naturally deviations in real-world research practice. Every CBR project is unique and faces its own set of challenges. Therefore, not every project is able to fully realize all of the principles that are reviewed (nor should they), and this does not diminish their contributions. My goal is simply to review these principles so that researchers who wish to engage in transdisciplinary approaches to CBR are best able to think through these fundamental conceptualization and design issues, create priorities that best serve their projects, and reflexively consider and report on their efforts. I should also note that there is a huge body of literature on the principles of community-based research which I cannot replicate here. This is merely a brief overview of the core principles of CBR which when taken seriously can facilitate transdisciplinarity.

Collaboration

Collaboration is vital in any community-based research project. Creswell (2003) suggests CBR centers on the "mutual creation of knowledge" (quoted in Pinto 2009, 933). There is, however, a continuum on which collaboration occurs. The extent of collaboration and the phases in which collaboration occurs can vary greatly from project to project. The higher the level of collaboration throughout a project the greater likelihood that disciplinary borders will be transcended and the project will become transdisciplinary. In other words, a transdisciplinary approach to CBR demands high levels of collaboration. Ideally, the entire process involves deep levels of collaboration between the researcher(s) and community partners. This includes problem identification, conceptualization and planning, data collection and interpretation, and the dissemination of the research results—including (co)authorship. This level of collaboration requires clearly determining, dividing and balancing roles, responsibilities and resources (Pinto 2009). Pinto provides the following definition of research collaboration: "social processes in which research- ers share roles and responsibilities with CBO personnel to accomplish tasks such as recruitment, data collection, interviews, supervising staff, data analysis, and writing and presenting results" (p. 934).

When thinking through issues of collaboration it is important to remember that community identified needs should be at the center of the research. Stoecker advocates developing "community-generated research questions" (2008, 50). Worthington (2007) notes, "CBR is systematic inquiry that incorporates a substantial level of community participa- tion for the purposes of community improvement and social change" (p. 480). When the issues and problems are identified on this basis then the research is likely to transcend any particular disciplinary vision. Stoecker (2008) urges researchers to balance their needs with those of the community they are serving. In this way CBR can bridge the acad- emy and the community. Pinto (2009) suggests that when working with a community-based organization it is also important to integrate the mis- sion of the CBO into the research. In these ways researchers can attempt to achieve "partnership synergy" (Lasker, Weiss & Miller 2001). Again, these kinds of synergistic practices are fundamental to the practice of transdisciplinarity.

In order to better understand the complexity of collaboration let's take a closer look at Pinto's (2009) HIV prevention research which explores the relationship between researchers and community-based organizations. Given the range of social stigmas and stereotypes associ- ated with HIV/AIDS, as well as the ability to prevent new infections, this kind of community-based work is particularly important. Pinto collected qualitative interview data from twenty informants working at ten differ- ent community-based organizations. Five of the CBOs involved in the study provided primarily medical HIV related services, and the other five CBOs provided primarily social HIV related services (including counsel- ing, prevention workshops, etc.).

The community-based organizations collaborated with academ- ics, physicians, individuals with PhD's in public health, psychologists, and social workers. It is important to note that the CBOs in this study are transdisciplinary by design, as are many community-based organi- zations. The composition of many CBO partners, therefore, facilitates the development of transdisciplinary approaches to community-based research if the professional/academic researchers are committed to transdisciplinary values. Pinto sought to ascertain CBO perspectives on making community-based health research more collaborative in order to aid disease prevention and intervention initiatives. Bear in mind that the major criticism of community-based research centers on an imbalance in power, resources and rewards, *systematically favoring academic/research institutions* who initiate research over their community partners. Pinto's research, which emphasizes *the perspectives of community-based organizations* on the CBR process, is of the utmost importance as we move towards merging CBR principles with transdisciplinary vision in an attempt to best address real-world issues and problems.

Pinto's main findings fall into four broad categories. First, Pinto found that researchers' personal characteristics impact the effectiveness of CBR projects from the point of view of community-based organizations. Ideally, researchers are highly collaborative, experts in the field, have an understanding of the community that is served by the CBO, and are sincere in their efforts. Second, partners working at the community-based organizations were concerned with the characteristics of the researchers' institutions. They favored institutions with positive reputations and scientific resources. Third, the study detailed the major characteristics of collaborative research which include: the research should improve services at the CBO, the research should have a purpose defined by all partners which should be an agreed-upon issue that is relevant to all parties, the research should involve participants and enhance their lives, the research should involve CBO staff at multiple stages of the research and the research should increase the knowledge base of the CBO staff and create avenues for professional development while also decreasing the knowledge gap between the researchers and CBOs (2009, 938–939). Finally, the interview data emphasized the importance of the community partner-researcher relationship. Important aspects of this relationship include: getting to know each other/relationship-building, the researcher getting to know the work of the CBO on a meaningful level, resolving social and professional tensions, dealing with differences instead of brushing them off (for example education, research experience, practical skill sets, etc.), and finding common ground (2009, 939).

The lessons learned in this research can be applied to community-based research collaboration with community-based organizations that deal with a range of topics inside and outside of HIV or health more broadly (for example, homelessness or domestic violence). Additionally, although established CBOs are unique in that they have their own infrastructure, organization, methodological practices, and budgetary issues, the data in this study are useful in thinking through issues that may arise when any researcher or research team are working with others (whether those others are community members, professionals/practitioners, or researchers from other disciplines)—although they may emerge in different forms, the same issues of collaboration, tension, and respect must be dealt with in any kind of team research.

Cultural Sensitivity, Social Action and Social Justice

It is important to remember that community-based research has a moral imperative. In other words, there is a social justice and social action undercurrent to community-based research projects. In this regard there are a host of ethical issues at play. For example, one must ask:

- Whose interests are being served by the research?
- How have community needs been identified?
- How are issues of power being dealt with throughout the process?
- Is the researcher or research team reflexive about issues of power, authority and ownership?
- Is the research sensitive to the community's cultural definitions and understandings?
- How collaborative is the conceptualization process in which definitions and understandings are agreed upon?
- What issues may arise when working with disenfranchised or marginalized populations?
- How can we work ethically, morally, respectfully and effectively with people who may be different from us?

Summarizing these issues Stoecker writes: "The ideal research project is one that serves community-identified needs, is sensitive to the cultural understandings of the community, and supports action around some community-identified issue" (2008, 50). The more researchers are willing to emphasize community needs for the betterment of the communities they aim to serve, the more researchers will be able to transcend their disciplinary training and bring together all available resources in order to most effectively address the issue or problem at hand. Therefore, attending to the social justice imperative of community-based research also facilitates transdisciplinarity.

Recruitment and Retention

Recruitment and retention often prove challenging in community-based research. These issues should be built into grant proposals as they may require both time and funds (Loftin, Barnett, Bunn & Sullivan 2005). Multiple recruitment strategies may need to be used (Loftin et al. 2005). In order to be able to effectively recruit research participants and retain them for the duration of the project it is important to make sure there has been in-depth community involvement in the research design process. Community understandings, norms and values should permeate the conceptualization process. This will allow researchers to effectively recruit participants and help to gain their trust so that they will be more likely to continue to participate. Moreover, if culturally sensitive definitions are used then participants are more likely to see their continued participation as valuable to themselves and to their community. Therefore, issues of insider and outsider statuses must be dealt with and not disavowed. Based on their community-based health research with African-Americans, Loftin and colleagues offer the following example:

> Culturally competent strategies for recruiting African-Americans might include posters and flyers illustrated with African-Americans posted in doctors' offices, clinics, churches, hairdressers, and barber shops; direct phone calls from African-American outreach workers; health fair screenings; presentations at African-American churches and/or barbershops with demonstrations of the intervention; public service announcements, especially on radio stations with a large black following; advertisements in church bulletins; and quotes from "satisfied customers." (2005, 256)

When thinking through issues of recruitment and retention the value of a transdisciplinary approach is clear. If the goal is to effectively address the issue or problem at hand, and community participation is vital towards reaching that goal, then the needs of the community will supersede the disciplinary perspective of the researcher or research team and ideally foster transdisciplinarity. An issue- or problem-centered approach creates a research context where different forms of scientific, experiential and lay understandings are tapped for their usefulness.

At this point it is important to emphasize that the principles of collaboration, cultural sensitivity and retention are all intimately linked. As alluded to an excellent example comes from Loftin and colleagues' (2005) research on diabetes prevention in rural African-American communities.

These projects were designed, in part, to address underrepresentation in research which the literature indicated was due to "historical mistrust of biomedical research, lack of cultural relevancy and competency, and less access to care" (Loftin et al. 2005, 252). The research team was highly reflexive about dealing with prejudice either as outsiders or, in the case of African-American researchers, as insider-outsiders (Loftin et al. 2005). The main goal of both diabetes studies was to determine effective approaches to recruitment and retention, which meant building "culturally competent approaches" and dealing with ethically charged issues of trust, incentives, and follow-up (Loftin et al. 2005).

The first study was a feasibility study that addressed the issue of culturally competent/sensitive intervention (in this case a dietary self-management intervention that helped people to help themselves). The dietary self-management intervention consisted of three sequenced components: 1) four dietary education classes lasting ninety minutes each, 2) two monthly discussion groups lasting sixty minutes each, and 3) nurse case manager follow-up by weekly telephone calls and one home visit. The retention strategies employed used value-based information and included reminders and incentives. Loftin and colleagues provide a robust explanation of *culturally competent/sensitive approaches* in relation to their research:

> Culturally competent characteristics of the intervention reflect the beliefs, values, customs, food patterns, language, and health care practices of Southern, rural African-Americans and seek to integrate these values into healthy dietary strategies. First, the intervention focused on the most meaningful and relevant topic reported by African-Americans in previous research, dietary education. Meals or snacks of typical ethnic food preferences were served at each screening and intervention session to integrate black cultural traditions associated with food. Participation of family members was encouraged to capitalize on the value of family and to provide transportation. Experiential learning approaches, such as participation in a cooking class, were used because they are the primary mode of learning for this population. Peer-professional discussion groups facilitated cultural translation of contents and culturally competent learning methods, such as story-telling. (Loftin et al. 2005, 253)

This project was highly successful because of the in-depth inclusion of community beliefs and values during all phases of the study. Similarly, the second study called "soul food light: preliminary test of the intervention" also yielded positive results (this study included longitudinal pretest and post-test effects of the intervention).

Loftin and colleagues (2005) note that several factors directly contributed to their success:

- getting the support of key stakeholders (including those in the medical community who were advising their patients to participate);
- gaining the trust of the community and building on existing relationships to do so;
- following the principles of mutuality;
- using respected members of the community in key roles in the research;
- valuing the advice of insiders who are trusted members of the community;
- actively demonstrating caring (the follow-up stage in the research was a critical part of this);
- building follow-up into the research design in order to intervene as problems may emerge (and demonstrate caring).

In terms of providing meaningful incentives for participation, the principles of CBR were again followed successfully. For example, the research team (including both the researchers and community partners) demonstrated the value they were contributing to the community, offered participants formal recognition, and used monetary and other financial prizes (such as gift cards) to encourage continued participation. The researchers also facilitated participation by building solutions to practical barriers into the study. For example, participant transportation was factored into the study (i.e., gas coupons for participants).

Building Trust and Rapport

Building trust and rapport with community members, research participants and CBO personnel is vital in community-based research. In order to retain research participants and yield successful outcomes it is important to continually nurture research relationships. The idea of "research" may be poorly received by members of some communities (Meade, Menard, Luque, Martinez-Tyson & Gwede 2009). This may be especially true when working with disenfranchised or marginalized populations (Meade et al. 2009). Again, the importance of including the community during research conceptualization and design (as well as during all other phases of the research) is vital. When the community helps shape the potential outcomes and lasting benefits of the research, they will feel more included, valued and empowered. This is an important way to build trust. It is equally important that the relationships researchers build in the community are genuine. Researchers must demonstrate their caring, interest and concern in order to cultivate reciprocal partnerships (Meade et al. 2009).

Multiplicity, Different Knowledges, Participation and Empowerment

Transdisciplinary approaches to community-based research require that a multiplicity of knowledges/ways of knowing are incorporated and valued. Participants in the community, CBO partners, and researchers will all bring different assumptions to bear on the research process. Additionally, all partners will bring different kinds of knowledge—experiential, scientific, and lay—to the project. It is likely that different partners will also bring different skill sets to the project. These different kinds of assumptions, knowledge, and experience must be respected and valued. Strand, Marullo, Cutforth, Stoecker, and Donahue write:

> This means that people's daily lives, achievements and struggles are no longer at the margin of research but are placed firmly at the center. CBR requires acknowledging the validity of the local knowledge generated in and through practice in community settings and weighing this alongside institutionalized, scientific, and scholarly professional knowledge familiar to faculty and students. (2003, 11)

Research partners should be willing to learn from one another and willing to teach one another. Pinto (2009) suggests that the most effective projects balance scientific and lay knowledge. When these forms of knowledge are viewed as complementary the research is more likely to be useful to both the community and the researcher(s) (Pinto 2009). Mutually beneficial research is likely to generate higher levels of commitment from all partners. Participatory research designs are often used in transdisciplinary community-based research because they may offer greater community control over the project (Stoecker 2005), and therefore they invite a multiplicity of understandings and renderings to emerge from the research process.

An outstanding example of incorporating different perspectives into a CBR study is the landmark study on community development and segregation that occurred in Chicago in 1986. Although at the time the research team referred to their efforts as "interdisciplinary," in retrospect I think it is safe to label this hallmark study "transdisciplinary." The research objectives were "to document progress made in fair housing work, evaluate ongoing fair housing programs, and identify factors related to the persistence of segregation in some areas. The goal was to further the development of fair housing as an integral part of healthy communities" (Lukehart 1997, 48.). In order to carry out this research a transdisciplinary team was assembled. The team included The Leadership Council for Metropolitan Open Communities (a Chicago-based fair housing organization that began in the 1960s) as well as twelve academic researchers and several members of the Chicago Area Fair Housing Alliance (CAFHA) (Lukehart 1997, 47).

The team of the CBO professionals, activists, academic researchers and community members was actively involved during all phases of the research. Initially the large team participated in a series of meetings to discuss issues and identify research needs (Lukehart 1997). This process led to the development of nine research projects, and due to the impressive and diverse group of people brought into the project the research received considerable funding (Lukehart 1997), illustrating how including a multiplicity of perspectives and knowledges may be viewed as a strength to external groups and can thus be used to garner research support (chapter 6 concludes with a return to this issue). Methodologically, the large group broke down into transdisciplinary subgroups, each comprised of academic and community stakeholders that organized around each of the nine projects (Lukehart 1997). Each team identified its research issue and determined an appropriate methodology; however, the larger group was used as a "sounding board" throughout the process (Lukehart 1997, 48). Research teams relied on a variety of methods, including census data, policy analysis, structured interviews, unstructured interviews, document analysis and participatory evaluation research (1997). In order to continue the process of rich collaboration and multiplicity each research team drafted a report about their findings which was distributed to the entire team for feedback (Lukehart 1997). The group then held a conference at the University of Chicago and invited additional stakeholders—such as members of government, community leaders and activists—to offer feedback (Lukehart 1997). This responsive process of feedback loops led to the writing of the final reports.

This research embodies the best of transdisciplinary cooperation as academic, lay and activist knowledge and experience were brought to bear during all phases—from identifying issues to determining research protocols—and feedback was systematically sought throughout the process. This project serves as an example of how evaluating multiple and diverse knowledge bases, coupled with a participatory approach, can foster highly successful transdisciplinary collaborations.

Community-based research has the potential to empower participants as well. Empowerment can occur in a host of ways, such as through educating participants on areas of interest or concern, providing wanted behavioral intervention strategies, and providing participants an opportunity to have their perspectives and experiences valued and validated in the knowledge-building process. Participatory approaches lend themselves to these forms of empowerment and should be considered when appropriate. The 1986 Chicago-based community development project illustrates how including relevant stakeholders during all phases of the research empowers community members, who, in that case, became agents of social change within their communities, even impacting public policy.

Flexibility and Innovation

Community-based research requires flexibility and innovation, issues which are heightened in a transdisciplinary effort where multiple resources and viewpoints are brought together in a problem-centered capacity. Things do not always go according to plan with these kinds of projects, and researchers must be willing to adapt to circumstances as they emerge. In transdisciplinary research the issue or problem at hand remains at the center of conceptualization processes and methodological decision-making. This means that the research design may need to be evaluated and revised throughout the research process. As noted earlier, it is for this reason that transdisciplinary research typically follows a recursive research design (Pohl et al. 2007). This can be particularly challenging in CBR because there are so many different partners who need to collaborate throughout the research process. All partners need to be open to adapting to new information and circumstances for the success of the project. Moreover, innovative approaches to problem-solving should be cultivated.

The need for flexibility and innovation, however, must be balanced against the need for structure. In this way transdisciplinary approaches to research create a paradox; they require both openness and structure. While all partners must be open to adaptation, it is vitally important that roles and responsibilities are clearly delineated. Ideally, the division of labor will receive considerable attention from the research partners prior to the commencement of the conceptualization and data collection or intervention process. Partners should all agree on, and understand, their roles and responsibilities within the project. As new situations emerge that may change the division of labor, partners should again convene (ideally in person but at minimum via telephone or email) to come to a new, modified arrangement based on unexpected changes. It is important that the structure of the project is created in a collaborative process and checked throughout the process so that all partners' expectations are met.

Representation and Dissemination

The representation and dissemination of research results is challenging in community-based research and transdisciplinary research (in any genre), so this issue is greatly heightened in transdisciplinary approaches to CBR. There are multiple issues to consider.

First, it is important that the research results have the potential to positively impact the community that was involved in the project. Typically, traditional academic writing is of little value to anyone outside of academia (an issue in and of itself that points to the need for new approaches to knowledge-building). The public has little to no access to academic journals, the format of academic writing is exclusive and prohibitive (i.e., filled with jargon), and the timeframe for academic publication doesn't allow for the rapid dissemination of research findings to the community that participated in the study. Therefore, it is important to disseminate research results through "alternative" channels which may include:

- brochures/informational pamphlets distributed at local organizations, business, schools, religious centers or CBOs
- radio broadcasts
- Internet postings
- stories in local newspapers
- presentations at public meetings or in community locations
- other venues likely to reach the target audiences

The importance of disseminating research findings in appropriate venues is evident in the example of the Chicago-based community development research noted earlier. As mentioned, the team presented preliminary findings at a local conference that they organized and to which they invited many non-academic stakeholders. Additionally, the team held a press conference during which they presented their findings to the media and public (Lukehart 1997). Given the group's desire to impact public policy regarding fair housing and segregation, and to include the public in their own development process, inviting the media into the process was vital. In this regard, the press conference had the double effect of educating the public and putting pressure on local government in order to promote positive social change.

It is also important to consider new or "alternative" forms of representation. For example, some transdisciplinary researchers turn to arts-based forms of representation which have the potential to reach and resonate with larger audiences, break-down stereotypes and build critical consciousness. Arts-based forms of representation are reviewed in the next chapter but may include:

- theatrical performances
- musical or dance performances
- poetry or spoken word readings
- documentary film screenings
- visual art or photography displays
- online photoblogs
- other forms

Next, it is important to consider issues of authorship. While differing from traditional academic research, in CBR the community (theoretically) may "own" the results, at least from an ethical stance (Strand et al. 2003). Put differently, in a CBR project the relevant community has a major stake in the research process. For example, findings may have the potential to impact the community's development process, healthcare opportunities, or access to educational services. There may be public policy implications as well. Therefore, does the community have the right to determine how results are used? Typically, researchers retain the ability to represent and disseminate research findings at their discretion; however, the expectations of all parties must be fleshed out and negotiated. This is much more complicated in research practice.

- Who gets to represent the research?
- Who gets to disseminate the results?

Group research efforts carry many challenges in this regard. It is very important to come to understandings about these issues prior to beginning the research process. This is another area where all partners' expectations should be stated and discussed, and then a plan should be agreed upon. There are many issues to consider here. First, researchers from different disciplines may have different disciplinary norms for publication and authorship (including the ability to produce co-authored versus single authored works, given tenure, promotion and funding constraints). If more than one researcher is working on the project, the team will have to decide what data/results are "common property" that any team members can write about (and if there are any restrictions on acceptable publication venues, citing the group work, and so forth) and what, if any, data/results "belong" to any individual team member. Questions to consider include:

- What are the expected co-authored outcomes of the project?
- Where will co-authored outcomes be published/disseminated?
- How will the writing and editing process occur in ways that are fair to all partners?

Even if there is only one researcher, he or she will have to work this out with the community partners. For instance, when an individual researcher or team of researchers works with a CBO, all of the same issues of authorship and co-authorship must be addressed. All of this needs to be considered carefully in a collaborative context.

Additional issues to consider include:

- What rights do the research participants have to represent and/or disseminate research results?
- How will issues of "the team" be dealt with/noted?
- What expectations does each partner have?
- How will issues of informed consent, confidentiality and anonymity be dealt with, particularly when researchers from different disciplines and CBO partners may have very different norms regarding these issues?

Table 4.1 Summary of CBR Principles and Design Issues in Transdisciplinary Research

Principles	Methodologically Enacting the Principles
Collaboration	Multidisciplinary teams comprised of differently positioned stakeholders with different perspectives and experiences. Deep levels of collaboration during all phases of the research.
Cultural Sensitivity, Social Action, Social Justice	Cultural understandings are valued and community identified needs are determined. Research has a social action agenda and social justice undercurrent.
Recruitment and Retention	Culturally competent approaches to recruiting participants for the duration of the study.
Building Trust and Rapport	Genuine and respectful relationships are built (and valued as vital for retention and successful outcomes).
Multiplicity and Different Knowledges	Different ways of knowing are incorporated and valued during all phases of the research. Participatory designs are used when appropriate.
Flexibility and Innovation	Recursive research designs and problem-centered methodologies are employed reflexively, making time and space for feedback and modifications.
Representation and Dissemination	Research findings reach relevant audiences through creative representational formats and the use of appropriate "alternative" venues for distributing findings.

Policy Implications

The research examples cited throughout this chapter show the possible connections between community-based research and policy-making that positively impact the affected communities. For example, policies regarding public school lunches have received considerable media attention in recent years as a result of dramatic increases in childhood obesity. Community-based research projects, such as the development and subsequent testing of a culturally competent food intervention in rural African-American communities, can yield important data about how to best create policies that serve local populations.

Of course, impacting the policy making process is difficult at best; however, it is an important extension of many CBR practices. Social/public policies are political and power-laden (Wedel, Shore, Feldman & Lathrop 2005). They are plans of action that may carry widespread consequences for the communities that they impact (Wedel et al. 2005). Unfortunately, as policies are often politically motivated, the publics they most affect are often left out of the process. Community-based research has the potential to uniquely impact policy making, particularly when conducted from a transdisciplinary approach. Due to their social action and social justice imperatives, many community-based research projects are undertaken with the goal of contributing to policies that impact the communities at hand. This is clear in the example of development and fair housing practices in Chicago.

Policies typically deal with how the state relates to local populations/communities (Wedel et al. 2005), making the need for community involvement obvious. In order to participate in policy-making processes the public needs to be engaged in shaping the policy agenda (McTeer 2005). In order for this to occur the public needs to be both informed and engaged (McTeer 2005). CBR is an avenue for creating this kind of engaged populace. Moreover, CBR can generate data that can be used to lobby for changes in current policies. In this regard it is important to bear in mind that "policy makers create and implement policy out of or along with, *already existing* programmes" (Carlsson 2000, 202). Therefore, CBR projects can be designed to examine the impact of current policies on particular communities and how those policies can be improved for the public good.

By adopting transdisciplinary approaches to CBR, the issue or problem remains at the center of the inquiry. Moreover, all available resources will be tapped in order to most effectively serve the research purpose. Finally, by amassing a wider range of intellectual capital, researchers are more likely to develop persuasive research reports that they and their community partners can use to lobby for community-centered change.

Cross-Cultural Projects and Transnational Research Collaborations

Research challenges are compounded and new challenges emerge when multi-disciplinary research teams are conducting studies in multiple countries and settings. In addition to the issues that occur whenever a multi-disciplinary research team is working together in a transdisciplinary effort (such as coming from different research paradigms, building respect and rapport, determining the division of labor and clearly setting up goals and responsibilities, and so forth), transnational research raises additional practical and ethical issues (for example, language barriers).

Treloar and Graham (2003) provide two examples of transdisciplinary health studies projects conducted in transnational settings. The first study, conducted by the International Clinical Epidemiology Network (INCLEN) on the cross-cultural context of obesity occurred in five (mostly developing) countries: Australia, Cameroon, Egypt, India, and Indonesia. The research team employed focus groups in order to "explore the personal, interpersonal, organizational, and societal influences on diet, body image, and physical activity" (2003, 925). The team was made up of researchers primarily from the social sciences but different disciplines who were a part of a long-standing international network. A range of practical issues emerged, such as language training, unreliable e-mail and fax communications systems at the different research sites, developing a theoretical framework for the study (a challenge in transdisciplinary research), and different levels of expertise in qualitative research (Treloar & Graham 2003).

Although there were many successful aspects of this study, it is important to consider some of the challenges the researchers faced in order to learn from their experience. For example, they dealt with discrepancies in ethical standards between the medical scientists and the social scientists (for instance, regarding when informed consent was needed). The researchers also had different levels of experience with interviewing (both data collection and analysis) which made data comparison across the sites problematic (Treloar & Graham 2003). There were also issues with respect to funding and technology (Treloar & Graham 2003). For example not all of the focus group interviews were recorded due to a lack of available recording technology (Treloar & Graham 2003). There were also disparities regarding how to translate the data (given the different languages the raw data was in), and unfortunately no uniform approach was agreed upon. Therefore, some sites translated the coded data and summaries while other sites just translated summaries (Treloar & Graham 2003). This failure points to the need for additional funding for bilingual staff members in transdisciplinary transnational projects. Otherwise, bilingual staff members may be overburdened with work, and there may be a failure to translate and transcribe the data in a uniform and thus comparable way.

Despite these challenges the researchers did develop a transdisciplinary conceptual framework which allowed for a systematic coding and analysis procedure. Treloar and Graham explain this procedure as follows: "The Australian investigator used the three topic areas (diet, body image, and physical activity) and the four levels of the conceptual framework (personal, interpersonal, organizational, and societal) to explore patterns across the five data sets. The results of this process were distributed to investigators at each site for comment" (2003, 928).

The second study Treloar and Graham (2003) review, conducted by the International Study of Perioperative Transfusion (ISPOT), used a mixed method survey and interview approach in a health technology assessment study in ten developed countries: Australia, Canada, Denmark, France, the Netherlands, Israel, Japan, Scotland, Spain, and the United States. The research team consisted mainly of medical scientists; however, qualitative researchers were located in two sites. Differing from INCLEN, these researchers were not a part of an established research team and came together only for this project and did not spend time developing a truly transdisciplinary theoretical framework, which greatly minimized the positive outcomes from this study. There was also a range of issues regarding different levels of funding and different levels of commitment, determining publishing formats, differential expertise and experience that were not dealt with collaboratively.

Together, these two studies show what is possible in transnational research while also pointing to the challenges. I suggest that the development of a transdisciplinary perspective during initial planning and coming together, and a focus on maintaining a transdisciplinary approach, would have enhanced each of these projects. This was the case in the "Household, Gender and Age Project" reviewed in chapter 3. The research team, spanning eight continents, devoted ample time to project development, particularly building the conceptual structure, and as a result the process yielded many successes.

Chapter Five

Arts-Based Research Practices

Designing Research That Is Useful for the Public

Here in the union of arts, humanities, and science, finally, we find the true origin of all encompassing wisdom. Wisdom is often transitory. *It may be experienced just as brief glimpses or flashes of revelations that reveal eternal insights and lead to moments of comprehension. Such mental experiences have enormously stimulated the development of all human activities from the arts to religion, and to science.*

—Richard R. Ernst (2000, 127)

Arts-based research (ABR) practices emerged from the 1970s to1990s[1] and now constitute a significant methodological genre (Sinner et al. 2006).[2] Arts-based research developed out of a confluence of factors including but not limited to: the effects of the social justice movements of the 1960s and 1970s, the rise in autobiographical data across the social sciences, critical theoretical perspectives, advances in embodiment theory, and moves towards public scholarship (Leavy 2009). Technology has further propelled advances in ABR via innovations including digital imaging, digital cameras, the Internet, PhotoShop, sound files and so forth. With respect to moves towards public scholarship, it is here that I think arts-based research may have the greatest potential to facilitate transdisciplinarity and thereby address real-world issues and problems of import.

As I noted in an earlier work, arts-based research has developed in a transdisciplinary methods context involving the crossing of disciplinary borders as well as cross-disciplinary collaborations (Leavy 2009). It is important to note that while ABR practices developed in a transdisciplinary methods context, not every inclusion of "art" in a research project qualifies as a transdisciplinary enterprise. In order for a project to be transdisciplinary the same principles noted throughout this book must be present in some combination: the bringing in of multiple disciplinary sources, holistic approaches to research, responsive methodological strategies, and so forth. With this said, I define arts-based research practices as

> a set of methodological tools used by qualitative researchers across the disciplines during all phases of social research including data collection, analysis, interpretation, and representation. These emerging tools adapt the tenets of the creative arts in order to address social research questions in holistic and engaged ways in which theory and practice are intertwined. Arts-based methods draw on literary writing, music, performance, dance, visual art, film, and other mediums.... Although a set of methodological tools, this genre of methods also comprises new theoretical and epistemological groundings that are expanding the qualitative paradigm. (Leavy 2009, 2–3)

For social researchers the appeal of the arts is in their ability to transform consciousness, refine the senses, promote autonomy, raise awareness, and express the complex feeling-based aspects of social life (Eisner 2002, 10–19). Arts-based research also draws on the oppositional, subversive, transformational, and otherwise resistive capabilities of the arts.

Free from academic jargon and other prohibitive barriers, the arts have the potential to reach a broad cross-section and to be both emotionally and politically evocative for these diverse audiences. The arts, at their best, can move people to see things in new ways. This is because the arts connect with people in sensory ways—reaching people on a level of humanness which extends far beyond the reach of the confines of any one discipline. Moreover, the arts can promote dialogue which cultivates understanding or critical consciousness, can problematize dominant ideologies, and can unsettle stereotypes. In these ways and others arts-based research practices can be used in community-based research projects, for example, as a means of sparking conversation and mutual learning. The capability of artistic forms to convey information to public audiences in understandable and even resonant ways makes ABR useful as a representational vehicle in many kinds of transdisciplinary projects, particularly when the research results in multiple outcomes, as is generally the case.

There are a range of genres of arts-based research that draw on different artistic practices. The genres of ABR include, but are not limited to:

- narrative inquiry
- fiction, literary and experimental forms of writing
- poetic inquiry
- the dramatic/performing /theatre arts
- music
- dance and movement
- visual art and photography
- audiovisual arts and film
- other mediums or combinations of mediums

While numerous methods within any of the genres can be employed in service of transdisciplinary goals, in this chapter I focus on examples from theatre arts. Recent research in this genre has signaled great potential to address issues of import. At times performance-based practices are also highly congruent with the goals of community-based research. (For a full discussion of the major ABR genres please see my book *Method Meets Art: Arts-Based Research Practice* 2009.)

Transdisciplinary approaches to research allow researchers to produce useful knowledge that addresses real-world issues or problems. In recent years there has been a rapid increase in research that employs practices that draw on theatre arts. I suggest these practices facilitate making research open to the publics we aim to serve and are therefore congruent with transdisciplinarity. Moreover, these practices require the merging of multiple disciplinary lenses (theatre arts, qualitative approaches to social research, and any number of disciplinary perspectives) in order to create something that exists beyond those disciplines. This set of research practices thus developed in a transdisciplinary environment and can be employed to further transdisciplinary visions.

Performances are accessible to diverse audiences and constitute an exchange or transfer between the audience and performer(s)/researcher(s). Moreover, the "exchange" may involve a complex negotiation of meanings (Leavy 2009). This interaction between the performer and audience also varies depending on the environment and mood (Langellier & Peterson 2006).

In social research, performance can serve many research purposes, including:

- consciousness-raising
- empowerment
- emancipation
- political agendas
- discovery
- exploration
- education
- information sharing

Though often considered a representational form, performance can be used as an entire research method, serving as a means of data collection and analysis as well as a (re)presentational form. Moreover, theories of performance are often entangled with methodological practices. Performance is therefore an investigation *and* a representation (Worthen 1998). McLeod (1988) suggests that there are five ways of making meaning (word, number, image, gesture, and sound) which Norris (2000) proposes are all integrated in drama. Performance methods are congruent with the *holistic views* of the research process that characterize transdisciplinarity. Methodologically, research-based plays can be created from data collected with traditional research methods, including, but not limited to, interviews, focus groups, large-scale quantitative surveys, and/or document analysis (Leavy 2009; Nisker 2008; Norris 2009).

Over the past few decades researchers in theatre arts, in collaboration with researchers across the disciplines, have pioneered multiple methods that rely on the dramatic arts, including:

- ethnodrama
- ethnotheatre
- performance ethnography
- performance texts
- playbuilding
- popular theatre
- health theatre
- "theatre of the oppressed"[3]
- Reader's theatre

I go into greater detail about playbuilding throughout this chapter as an example of these kinds of approaches because I believe that this approach draws on the tenets of both arts-based research and community-based research, and thus retains enormous potential to advance transdisciplinarity. For these and other reasons to be explicated I will suggest that playbuilding is necessarily a transdisciplinary approach to research.

Core Principles and Research Design Issues

In order to understand the potential of arts-based research as a transdisciplinary undertaking it is important to first review the core principles of ABR, which, as with community-based research, can actually vary greatly from project to project. I should also note that there is a large and rapidly emerging body of literature on arts-based research which I cannot replicate here. This is merely an overview of the core principles of ABR which when taken seriously can facilitate transdisciplinarity.

Creativity and Innovation

All things must change to something new, to something strange.
—Henry Wadsworth Longfellow

The recent growth in arts-based research practices across the social sciences, health studies and education has been propelled by qualitative researchers analyzing the similarities between scientific research and artistic practice. To do so, some have exposed the false polarization of art and social inquiry (see Saarnivaara 2003). For example, both scientific research and artistic practice are fuelled by creativity (Ernst 2000; Janesick 2001). In this regard, Janesick suggests the term "artist-scientists" (2001). Saldana (1999) rightly observes that both research and artistic practice require thinking conceptually, symbolically and metaphorically. Innovation, intuition and flexibility all play key roles in both the scientific and artistic communities. The principles underscoring these practices are thus the same. Moreover, both communities aim to discover, explore and illuminate. To summarize, key principles in both artistic and scientific practice include:

- thinking conceptually and building conceptual structures
- thinking symbolically

- using metaphors and metaphorical analysis
- innovation
- intuition
- flexibility
- discovering, exploring, illuminating

As I wrote in an earlier work, attention to creativity and innovation allows us to think in terms of "new research structures" (Leavy 2009, 258). Arts-based practices are on the methodological cutting-edge—researchers are "carving" new practices and creating "new ways to see" (Leavy 2009, 254). Methodologically, arts-based research practices lend themselves to innovation because the "incubation phase" of research, when ideas are generated and given space and time to percolate, is generally afforded significant attention in projects relying on ABR (Hunter et al. 2002). This may lead to the development of new ideas and approaches. Here another link between ABR and transdisciplinarity can be drawn out. Transdisciplinarity also fosters greater attention to early idea generation. For example, as noted in the last chapter transdisciplinary approaches to community-based research often demand extensive preparation time, allowing stakeholders to be brought together to share ideas, expectations and disciplinary perspectives. This often leads to a negotiation process and the emergence of new ideas. Here the example of playbuilding is illustrative.

The highly collaborative nature of playbuilding promotes great attention to idea generation and creativity. Playbuilding as research is the practice of collaboratively producing evocative texts which are performed (Barone 1990; Norris 2000, 2009; Tarlington & Michaels 1995). Joe Norris (2000, 2009) has worked extensively on developing this practice, so I draw considerably on his groundbreaking work.

Playbuilding is a topic, issue- or problem-centered research strategy (which is why I suggest it can serve transdisciplinary needs). This method involves assembling a group of people to discuss and research a topic of mutual interest (Norris 2009). Norris refers to this group of people as A/R/Tors, denoting actors-researchers-teachers and building on the A/R/tography (artist-researcher-teacher) framework developed by Irwin and de Cosson (2004). I suggest that in a transdisciplinary project not all of the collaborators would need to be actors nor would all need to participate in the performance. There may be many different ways to configure a given project drawing on the tenets of playbuilding while not following Norris's method prescriptively. Irrespective of how the group is ultimately configured, it is important to understand that all participants are stakeholders in the process—collaborators, partners, co-creators and co-authors (Norris 2009). This research strategy therefore raises similar issues with respect to collaboration as addressed earlier in regards to community-based research (which will not be repeated here), and thus I suggest that playbuilding merges the tenets of arts-based research and community-based research.

Once a research team of A/R/Tors is assembled the group brainstorms about the topic at hand. The group draws on autoethnographic observations and often data from other sources as well, including literature reviews, newspapers and/or fiction (Norris 2009). I suggest that in a transdisciplinary project the research team would *necessarily* conduct a literature review (bringing in multiple disciplinary perspectives) and may incorporate data found in numerous pre-existing sources or original data collected in any number of ways (e.g., interviews, surveys, document analysis). It is also possible that when applying a transdisciplinary approach the literature review could take center stage in the knowledge-building process and become the basis for the scripting process.

Over the past decade and a half the topic of bullying has received considerable attention from researchers and the national media in response to major incidents of school violence as well as more recent highly publicized incidents of bullying and cyber bullying that have led to a startling number of teen suicides. As noted in earlier chapters, this problem has many different components, for example:

- psychological
- sociological
- technological (e.g., social networking, camera-phones, etc.)
- legal
- educational
- economic
- status characteristics (race, ethnicity, class, gender, sexuality, religion, physical/mental well-being)
- and others

Therefore, research that hopes to make progress towards dealing with this issue needs to be transdisciplinary by design. No one discipline holds the keys to combating bullying. A number of projects exploring bullying have been conducted via performance-based methods. From these studies we can learn strategies for incorporating ABR into large-scale transdisciplinary investigations of bullying. Here an excellent example comes from Norris's work on bullying.

Norris has been involved in the development of more than two hundred performance pieces through his group, "Mirror Theatre." The group has tackled numerous transdisciplinary topics including bullying. The program *"What's the Fine Line?"* presented a workshop and performance on bullying (Norris 2009). In order to create this program the team of A/R/Tors assembled and shared their own experiences regarding bullying. Then they drew on existing literature and a cross-national study conducted by Smith, Morota, Junger-Tas, Olweus, Catalano and Slee (1999, in Norris 2009). The study included data about girl-on-girl bullying which often occurs in changing rooms (Norris 2009). Female cast members (team members) shared their personal experiences about girl-on-girl bullying with the group (Norris 2009). From this combination of data and several discussions within the group about the data, the scene *"The Girls' Locker Room"* was created (Norris 2009).

It is important to acknowledge that the creativity and innovation promoted by ABR can, at times, also be the target of criticism from the larger scientific community. Some fear that innovation will lead to a free-for-all where "anything goes" and scientific standards fall by the wayside. In this vein Jones (2006) notes that "novelty" can make people "uncomfortable." However, the history of science and art is very much based on novelty—pushing and expanding the borders. Progress requires innovation. Progress demands continued exploration, discovery and creativity. I am reminded of the famous quote by Ramsay Clark: "Turbulence is life force. It is opportunity. Let's love turbulence and use it for change." The merging of transdisciplinary vision and arts-based practices has great potential to advance research agendas, but to do so we must be unafraid to innovate. I elaborate on these issues in the next chapter.

Holistic Approach with Evolving or Responsive Methodologies

At their best, arts-based research practices are employed as a part of a *holistic* or *integrated* approach to research (Hunter et al. 2002; Leavy 2009). When ABR is employed in a transdisciplinary project that is driven by transdisciplinary vision, it promotes this kind of holistic approach. As noted earlier, a holistic approach to research design explicitly links each phase of a research project, while merging theory with practice. Moreover, a holistic approach to research is a process-oriented view of research (Hesse-Biber & Leavy 2011; Leavy 2009). In this regard, the intuition and flexibility needed to foster ABR is enabled methodologically through evolving or responsive approaches to methodology (as reviewed in chapter 3). Transdisciplinary approaches to ABR can promote highly thoughtful, reflexive and responsive methodologies where new insights, new learning, unexpected data (and possibly ongoing group conversation) propel cycles of going back to re-analyze data and/or revise aspects of the research design as needed. Again, the methodological recursive process of playbuilding is illustrative. The playbuilding process typically goes as follows (as was evidenced in the example of "*What's the Fine Line?*"):

> First, is data collection (generation), followed by data analysis (interpretation), and concluded with dissemination (performance). Such is the case with ethnodrama, where data is traditionally collected, analyzed, and then disseminated through an "alternative" form of representation. With Playbuilding, data is generated and interpreted in a different manner, and, at times, these three phases are simultaneous. (Norris 2009, 22)

The outcome of playbuilding is a live performance which may in turn generate new data or interpretations of the data as audience members are brought into the process (Norris 2009). For example, post-performance discussions or focus groups can be used to generate new data for the next phase in a mixed or multi-method project (which transdisciplinarity often results in). Here, again, there is a clear parallel to the process that typically occurs in community-based research where new interpretations are generated through an iterative process.

Conceptual Issues, Multiplicity and Engaging Diverse Publics

There are innumerable transdisciplinary real-world issues and problems which arts-based research practices may be useful in addressing. For example, ABR has been used in projects about such topics as: Hunger (Thomas 2008); Race/racism/discrimination/prejudice (Denzin 2003; Gatson 2003; Norris 2009; Thomas 2008); Violence (Hershorn 2005; Norris 2009); Poverty (Diamond 2004); Health/health care (Bergum & Dossetor 2005; Gray, Fitch, Labrecque & Greenberg 2003; Locsin,

Barnard, Matua & Bongomin 2003; Mienczakowski 1994; Nisker & Bergum 1999; Picard 2000; Poindexter 2002); Eating disorders/body image/ the "body" (Chan 2003; Leavy 2010; Norris 2009; Snowber 2002); Trauma (Harvey, Mishler, Koenan & Harney 2000); Grief (Vickers 2002); and Bullying (Norris 2009; Thomas 2008). In all of these instances ABR facilitated the exploration, description or public understanding of a transdisciplinary topic of considerable import. Of course this list is far from exhaustive and is merely illustrative. With respect to facilitating transdisciplinary efforts, I think ABR offers three primary advantages.

First, ABR is particularly useful for accessing highly conceptual fundamental dimensions of social life (Sinner et al. 2006). For example, ABR can be used to get at feelings like grief, shame or love, which are core aspects of humanity. ABR can also be used to access attitudes that shape experience, such as bias, prejudice or compassion. One could easily argue these kinds of feelings and attitudes are aspects of topics such as poverty, violence, bullying, living with illness, and so on. For example, a photograph or other visual art installation may jar spectators into seeing an issue like racism or homophobia from different perspectives, forcing viewers to reflect on their own attitudes and assumptions. Similarly, an exhibit that expressly challenges stereotypes about gender roles or what a "family" looks like may propel viewers into (re)considering previously taken-for-granted assumptions. Therefore, holistic transdisciplinary approaches to these topics may aim to tap into these hard-to-get-at issues. ABR may be particularly useful in these circumstances.

Second, ABR opens up multiplicity in meaning-making instead of pushing authoritative claims. For example, a piece of visual art can be interpreted in different ways depending on the viewer (his or her attitudes, values and prior experiences) as well as the context of viewing. There is no one way to make sense of a piece of art. In this respect research-produced artworks can democratize meaning-making and decentralize academic researchers as "the experts." This may be important in transdisciplinary efforts considering that the stakes may be high for many different groups. Here we can turn to some examples of using performance-based methods in health studies.

Performance-based approaches to research are increasingly being employed in health research projects. Often these efforts involve goals ranging from educating the public to challenging stereotypes to exploring emergent ethical issues to including various groups (often disenfranchised groups) in health policy development. These projects typically necessitate bringing multiple stakeholders into the process and thus could be greatly enhanced by transdisciplinary approaches to research.

Some research-based plays tackle emergent ethical and moral health care issues. In these circumstances the performances can help bring together various differently situated stakeholders, including the public at large, to explore the human side of new scientific capabilities. For example, with funding from the Canadian Institutes of Health Research and Health Canada, Jeff Nisker (2008) wrote "Sarah's Daughters" about predictive genetic testing and "Orchids" about testing in vitro embryos for genetic markers. "Orchids" was performed sixteen times in English and French (Nisker 2008), indicating the potential for research-based plays to reach relatively large public audiences.

There are also research-based plays that explore issues like mental illness, such as Abi Bown's (2004) "Mind the Gap" (Nisker 2008). Projects like this often are a means of challenging stereotypes, curbing stigmatization and highlighting the need for effective public services. Jim Mienczakowski has been at the forefront of this kind of research, and so I elaborate on an example from his collaborative work.

Mienczakowski, Smith and Morgan (2002) developed a health theatre performance based on interviews conducted with people diagnosed with schizophrenia. The show was titled "Syncing Out Loud" (1992/1994) and enabled the audience to learn about the experience of schizophrenia from the perspective of the research participants who live with it. The performance challenged misconceptions and prejudices attributed to schizophrenia and mental disorders in general. Based on their experience in this area, Mienczakowski and colleagues assert that a performance-based methodology within health studies creates a space for the voices of marginalized health care recipients and caregivers (professional and personal). Theatre can therefore be used to access and present subjugated voices, to educate, and to confront and work through stereotypes and misunderstandings. Moreover, theatre has the potential to emancipate (Mienczakowski 1995). I believe that transdisciplinarity, as a guiding perspective, can further this potential as well as facilitate the tenets of community-based research as appropriate to a particular project.

There are considerable ethical issues to be mindful of. Health theatre is a form of *public performance*; therefore, the researchers bear responsibility for the impact the performance has with regard to audience well-being after the performance, just as qualitative researchers have an obligation to protect their informant's confidentiality and to leave informants and their environment unharmed (see Bailey 1996, 2007). The need to create ethical guidelines has arisen out of incidents in which audience members were put at risk as a result of witnessing an ethnodramatic performance (Mienczakowski, Smith & Morgan 2002).

Nisker suggests that various stakeholders should be given drafts of the script for feedback, "reality checks" and to uncover differing perspectives (2008, 619). This feedback piece, in some form, is necessary in transdisciplinary projects in order to actively engage with and negotiate multiple viewpoints. Mienczakowski and colleagues suggest having a preview performance with an audience of people who possess knowledge about the topic under investigation. They also note that "post-performance forum sessions" can be used to analyze audience responses to the performance, in order to assess the show's impact (2002, 49). This also seems vital in any kind of community-based research project where community members are being educated about a health care issue. During this session understanding/misunderstanding can be uncovered and addressed. As noted earlier, in many projects additional data is gathered post-performance, through a group conversation, focus groups or other debriefing/coming together formats and serves as an example of applying transdisciplinarity in arts-based research. Data unearthed during this time may inform future performances, other data collection and/or the findings or distribution of findings. Therefore, this phase of post-performance debriefing and/or data collection is a part of a responsive methodology. Nisker (2008) suggests taking a short break in between the performance and any post-performance dialogue so that audience members can begin to process new information and create some space from any immediate visceral reactions. In these ways, as researchers confront ethical issues, they also create measures for maximizing the credibility of the usefulness of the research.

Inviting stakeholders and/or community members into the drafting process as well as pre- and post-performance dialogue is more than an ethical safeguard. These phases surrounding a performance are opportunities for building trust and rapport with differently situated stakeholders. Likewise, the research team can negotiate their cross-disciplinary perspectives. These are therefore opportunities for building understanding. Further, in accord with a responsive and participatory approach to research, these times in the process create spaces for revision and (re)negotiation. In a CBR project these spaces may also serve to help combat potential retention problems. These phases are important opportunities for learning and validating differing viewpoints which in turn may inspire continued participation. In projects with a proactive educational component this may be particularly important.

These examples and ethical quagmires also highlight two tensions that may be present in ABR projects. Researchers have to deal with the ambiguity, or potential ambiguity, of art's messages (the multiple meanings that may emerge). First, this means researchers need to balance their needs to present specific interpretations of the data against the possibilities for multiple interpretations of the data to emerge. Second, researchers need to be ethically mindful of how various interpretations may impact research participants, those who are exposed to the art, and any broader implications (with respect to public policy and the like). This is tricky as all of the possible interpretations of a work of art can not necessarily be known in advance. However, strategies to apply include:

- bringing key stakeholders into the process
  ▷ Soliciting the input of differently positioned stakeholders and non-stakeholders at various points, cycling back and incorporating that feedback into the project
- sharing preliminary findings
  ▷ Soliciting feedback, debriefing with those who shared feedback and following-up with them

By using these strategies researchers can go a long way towards understanding the varied interpretations and implications of the work they are putting out, and, to some extent, determining how large the universe of possible meanings will be.

The issue of democratizing knowledge production and dissemination brings me to the third advantage of ABR: engaging diverse publics with the products of research. ABR can be used to extend public scholarship because it is free from prohibitive jargon and has a greater likelihood of being accessible to broad audiences. Here a clear connection between community-based research and arts-based research can be made. ABR can be used in a CBR project. This can occur in many ways.

For example, during idea generation the various stakeholders (researchers, CBO personnel, community members) can use "concept mapping" as a way of collaboratively building and negotiating their ideas and perspectives. To do so, all that would be needed would be a large poster board/large sheet of paper/whiteboard with color magic markers. The process might look like this:

- A major concept, issue or problem pertinent to the study could be written in black ink in the center of the sheet (such as "health intervention," "community violence" or "bullying").
- Then, group members could talk about connected concepts, issues and problems from their perspective. Different color markers could be used to extend out from the initial concept with the ideas generated in the group.
- Connections could be made between concepts. Depending on how much energy is invested in this process, solid or spotted lines could be used to denote the strength of relationships between concepts or problems.

This is just one example of how to implement a visual strategy during idea generation. This process may also serve as a team-building exercise in community-based research.

An arts-based method of data generation may also be used in a transdisciplinary CBR project. For example, playbuilding and other performative methods can be used to gather and/or interpret data. In this regard and as noted throughout this chapter, ABR is often employed as a part of a participatory research design (which again makes ABR congruent with the goals of some CBR projects). Finally, an arts-based form of representation may be used in a CBR project in order to disseminate the research findings to the communities of interest in resonant ways (such as an art exhibition in a local community center, art gallery or local businesses or a public performance). Arts-based forms of representation often function to raise critical consciousness and promote understanding and thus may be very useful in some CBR studies. Here an excellent example comes from Suzanne Thomas's research on bullying.

Suzanne Thomas (2008) used performance-based research as a part of a community-based arts education project aimed at studying bullying. This project brought together an academic researcher with pre-service teachers and community members. The group built a conceptual structure for the project that addressed issues of inequality. The project, titled *"Bullying Inside Out,"* culminated in a performance "in which teachers investigate emotional, physical, and psychological dimensions of bullying and explore the dynamics between the bully, bullied, and bystander.... Interweaving of role-playing, song, and dance... reveals multiple dimensions of bullying and its silent forms in cyber space" (Thomas 2008, 78). Such an approach to this topic could be used in a transdisciplinary investigation into bullying as a part of a mixed or multi-method approach. For example, a multidisciplinary team of researchers could conduct a transdisciplinary literature review and collect data via a large scale survey, a smaller sample of in-depth interviews and/or focus groups, and perhaps ethnographic observation (on school playgrounds, in school cafeterias, or online). Other stakeholders could be brought into the process, for example:

- parents
- teachers
- guidance counselors
- social workers
- school administrators
- after school programming staff members
- public school bus drivers
- local leaders
- and others

The script writing could serve as a part of idea generation and negotiation. The performance(s) could serve as part of the dissemination of the research findings (and could also be used to stimulate conversation during post-performance discussion or focus groups, which may result in the generation of additional data). Differing from academic prose, which is difficult for most people to read and understand, the performance could be geared towards a wide audience with respect to age, education and other relevant factors. Moreover, different performances could be targeted to different groups such as:

- students in elementary schools
- students in secondary schools
- students and peer leaders in college and university settings
- parents and PTO members
- teachers, guidance counselors and school social workers

- professors and college administrators
- community leaders and policy makers

Performances could occur in public school auditoriums, colleges or other accessible community locations.

Aesthetics

At their best the arts can be evocative, provocative, thought provoking, illuminating and even arresting. The arts can tap into dimensions of knowing and feeling that are hard to get at other ways and can draw people into seeing things differently. The arts can also provide joyful experiences where people's senses are heightened and they experience pleasure. However, it is important to acknowledge that this ideal is probably rarely met even in the art world. Rather, the aesthetic or *artful* quality of art exists on a continuum. When working with an arts-based approach to research it is important to be mindful of the *artfulness* of the resulting work. To do so one must pay attention to the craft from which he or she is borrowing (Leavy 2009). Transdisciplinarity has the potential to improve the artistic merit of arts-based research because cross-disciplinary expertise (from literature and/or collaborators) is brought into the process in a meaningful and sustained way. Arguably, this is yet another advantage of ABR—pushing researchers towards disciplinary cross-pollination. Despite the value of considering and attempting to achieve artistic merit, it is important to do so in relation to the goals of the study. This is not art simply for the sake of art, but rather is a part of a larger research project. The research issue or problem remains at the center of all practices.

Returning to the example of playbuilding we can see the role of "artfulness" at play. Playbuilding has to draw on the tenets of the dramatic arts in a meaningful way as it represents the data. Norris explains this part of the process as he reviews going from *data to drama*: "The A/R/Tors take the generated data and judiciously take artistic license, using metaphor, composites, and theatrical styles to create a verisimilitude of lived-experiences to create texts (theatrical vignettes) that evoke conversation" (2009, 35). In other words the tenets of dramatic script writing are employed, even though the raw data comes from personal, secondary, and empirical sources. Researchers can engage in a process of characterization, dialogue/monologue construction, plotting, storylining, and setting the scene (Saldana 1999). Moreover the group has to decide which moments to emphasize or draw out.

While some researchers suggest that art works created in social research must meet aesthetic and artistic criteria developed in the arts (for example, see Faulkner 2009), I disagree. While ideally research-driven artistic works are attentive to the craft they are adapting, they need not be "great" works of art per se in order to be useful (Leavy 2010). In transdisciplinary research, which is necessarily issue- or problem-centered, the issue is *usefulness*. The questions then are:

- What is your goal?
- Are the art works produced effective tools with respect to the research objectives?
- Has the research issue or problem stayed at the center of the ABR process? (The artistic qualities of the work should not supersede meeting the research objectives.)

Table 5.1 Summary Table of ABR Principles and Design Issues

Creativity and Innovation	Creativity, intuition and flexibility are employed. Researchers may build new research structures and new ways to see.
Holistic Approach with Evolving or Responsive Methodologies	Integrated approaches to research design that link theory and practice, and responsive or iterative methodologies that promote reflexivity.
Conceptual Issues, Multiplicity and Engaging Diverse Publics	Taps into hard-to-get-at issues (at times, highly conceptual topics), opens up meaning-making and can engage diverse publics through inclusiveness, inventive representational forms and multiple venues for the distribution of findings.
Aesthetics	Artfulness in relation to the usefulness of research findings for stakeholders, paying attention to the craft of the artistic practices used with usefulness in mind and creating evocative, provocative, illuminating and sensory representations of findings.

I suggest when evaluating research-driven art that researchers shy away from questions like "Is it a good piece of art?" and rather ask "What is this piece of art good for?" (Leavy 2010). The issue of aesthetics and artistic merit are briefly revisited in the next chapter during the discussion of evaluation.

Policy Implications

Augusto Boal has been at the forefront of promoting the political capabilities of theatre in his pioneering works *Theatre of the Oppressed* (1985) and *Legislative Theatre: Using Performance to Make Politics* (1998). Boal (1985) asserts that theatre is a highly effective political weapon that can educate, inform, and incite people to action.

There are many possibilities for how transdisciplinary approaches to research-based performance, or other forms of ABR, can be used to affect public policy. Primarily, the greatest potential centers on involving the public in the policy development process. Public policies are power-laden and develop in power-rich political contexts that may be masked as neutral (Wedel et al. 2005). Often various stakeholders are cut out of the policy development process (just as community members may be cut out of their own development processes). One of the persistently difficult challenges in policy research is developing effective strategies for citizen participation in policy development (Nisker 2008). Policy researchers need new tools for engaging the public in this process (Nisker 2008), including agenda setting (McTeer 2005). In this regard Nisker writes that "theater can be such an instrument, as it is able to engage, cognitively and emotionally, large numbers of citizens of diverse perspectives, provide them relevant information...and provide a forum where citizens are able to air and debate their opinions for policy research purposes" (2008, 614).

Performances created in a transdisciplinary context carry great potential to involve relevant stakeholders and the public more generally in the policy development process. First, transdisciplinarity requires bringing in multiple viewpoints. Second, participatory designs are often sought, as is the case in community-based research. Third, theater has the potential to:

- challenge stereotypes or jar people into thinking about an issue differently
- build bridges across differences

- access and illuminate differences
- inform and educate (by providing information or proactively intervening in a social problem)
- connect with people deeply thereby "reaching" them and helping them to feel invested in the issue

There are numerous examples of health policy researchers harnessing the power of performance to address major healthcare issues. Examples of plays created as tools for health policy development include a production titled "Practicing Democracy" written by Diamond in 2004 which explores how poverty impacts health; as noted earlier, a play titled "Mind the Gap" written by Bown in 2004 which explores mental illness; a play titled "Sarah's Daughters" written by Nisker in 2001 which explores the ethical issues relating to adult predictive genetic testing; and a play called "Orchids" also written by Nisker in 2001 which explores testing in vitro embryos for genetic markers (Nisker 2008). There are many other examples of using the possibilities of performance in this manner, including research-based plays about HIV/AIDS, breast cancer, dementia, and Alzheimer's disease to name a few (Nisker 2008).

Health policy researchers are actively drawing on the potential of the dramatic arts to engage and inform people in order to involve different segments of the public in the development of health policy (Nisker 2008). Nisker writes:

> Theatrical productions, focusing on the persons at the center of a health care issue, can bring all who ought to be responsible for its policy development (e.g., patients, their family members, the general public, health professionals) to a better understanding of the new scientific possibilities, ethical issues, and most important, the persons immersed therein. (2008, 615)

For example, beyond health care conditions per se, there are many contemporary ethical issues and questions emerging at the intersection of science and technology (McTeer 2005), such as in vitro embryo testing, stem cell research, cloning, and many other examples. These questions are transdisciplinary by nature and profoundly impact the public. Therefore, researchers must find ways to bring the public into these discussions in informed ways.

One could imagine how transdisciplinary performance-based studies on many different topics could be used to bring the public into the policy development process. For example, as a result of some highly publicized tragic incidents there has been a surge in public interest in issues surrounding school bullying and cyber bullying. Differently positioned stakeholders, including students, parents, teachers, school administrators, after school programming staff, school bus drivers and others, could be brought into the policy process through information sharing, agenda setting and creating documents detailing concerns and proposed remedies. The possibilities are limitless.

Chapter Six

Evaluation Strategies and the Future of Transdisciplinarity

*The dogmas of the quiet past are inadequate to the stormy pres-
ent. The occasion is piled high with difficulty, and we must rise
with the occasion. As our case is new, so we must think anew
and act anew. We must disenthrall ourselves.*

—Abraham Lincoln

Evaluation is a particularly thorny issue in transdisciplinary research
because no clear peer community has yet been firmly established
(Wickson et al. 2006). This does not mean, however, that researchers need to continually reinvent the wheel. Rather, there are various
strategies that researchers routinely employ in order to build credibility into their transdisciplinary efforts. In some instances, depending
on the goals of the study and the methodological design, conventional
measures are sought, such as validity, reliability, transferability, authen-
ticity, trustworthiness and the like, which may be applicable in some
combination. With this said, innovation is also occurring with respect
to issues of understanding, credibility and corresponding strategies for
evaluation. As would be the case within any research paradigm, I suggest that it is best to start to think about issues of evaluation in relation
to the tenets of transdisciplinarity.

Transdisciplinary research is necessarily issue- or problem-centered.
This means that all design issues should be determined in relation to the
specific issue or problem at hand. The development of a research strategy
should be driven by the research topics and purpose(s). Therefore, transdisciplinary research can largely be evaluated with respect to effectively

addressing the issue or problem at hand, staying focused on the research objectives, and using appropriate strategies to address the issue or problem (including bringing in relevant disciplinary expertise). Moreover, transdisciplinary research is intended to be useful, and thus *usefulness* is a major evaluative criterion.

Early in this book I referred to Wickson and colleagues (2006) who suggest that transdisciplinary research generally includes the following design features:

1. responsive goals (refining and shifting goals)

2. broad preparation (theory and literature from multiple disciplines)

3. evolving methodology

4. significant outcome (contribute to the solution of a problem, "satisfying multiple agendas" [p.1057])

5. effective communication

6. communal reflection (in addition to personal reflection) (pp. 1056–1057)

When figuring out how to build effective projects and evaluate those projects we have worked on or that others have worked on, it is helpful to return to the key design elements and determine how well they have been achieved.

In this regard it may also be helpful to return to the primary characteristics or concerns of transdisciplinarity in order to evaluate how well they have been realized. Various models were reviewed in the first chapter, including the following one put forth by Pohl and Hadorn: "1. the transcending and integrating of disciplinary paradigms 2. participatory research 3. the focus on life-world problems 4. the search for unity of knowledge beyond disciplines" (2007, 70).

Again, the models provided by the scholars noted may be adapted in any number of ways, and so evaluative claims should always be considered with respect to specific projects.

In this chapter I recap some of the primary strategies for strengthening transdisciplinary endeavors. In this regard I also review the major evaluation concepts by which transdisciplinary research may be assessed (beyond any traditional evaluation concepts used based on the specific disciplinary methods adapted for the project). As I suggest strategies for strengthening research and evaluating research, bear in mind how they respond to the general design features outlined by Wickson and colleagues and the criteria delineated by Pohl and Hadorn. Finally, I make some comments about the future of transdisciplinarity suggesting how the research community can continue to move forward in our knowledge-building practices. In this vein I note the major institutional challenges the research community faces while emphasizing reasons to be optimistic.

Summary of Strategies for Strengthening the Project

Responsiveness and Flexibility

Transdisciplinary research is designed to respond to an identified need or needs. In other words, transdisciplinarity is an orientation and approach that allows us to address real-world issues and problems. Transdisciplinary research design typically follows a responsive or iterative approach to methodology where there are built-in opportunities for reflection, renegotiation and revision as new insights warrant. A responsive approach to research design helps to ensure that the research problem and questions stay at the center of the research process. In this regard Nicolescu (2002) suggests that transdisciplinary researchers aim for rigor, opening and tolerance. Nicolescu posits that rigor is the result of perpetual search and opening refers to acceptance of the unknown (here we see a link between flexibility and innovation). A project can be evaluated, in part, based on how well the tenets of a responsive methodology have been followed. In this context flexibility and adaptation are viewed as strengths.

In order to effectively address the topic at hand and enact a responsive or iterative approach, researchers must be flexible during all stages of a project. For example, researchers and/or research partners must be open to finding methods, strategies and solutions that they may not be familiar with (through the use of literature, cross-disciplinary expertise and/or other assistance). Transdisciplinary research often involves multi-method or mixed methods designs which should be constructed in service of the research goals. Some questions to consider include:

- Has a responsive or iterative methodology been followed?
  - ▷ Has the research problem or issue remained at the center of the research process?
- Have the researchers been flexible and open throughout the process?
- Have the researchers adapted to new insights as appropriate?

Innovation and Creativity

As noted throughout this book transdisciplinarity requires innovation and creativity. This can occur in many different ways from how participants are recruited into projects to the mediums used for representation. Examples of issues to consider include:

- Has the issue or problem been considered from many different viewpoints?
- Have disciplinary sets of knowledge been combined in new ways and been put into service of the problem or issue?
  - ▷ In this regard, is the emergent conceptual framework innovative? Is the methodological approach creative, as needed, in order to address the problem effectively?
- Are the researchers/research partners willing to try new methods or strategies?
  - ▷ Are the researchers/research partners open to new understandings and approaches?
- Have appropriate technologies been put in service of addressing the problem (if relevant)?

Cross-Checking Preliminary Findings and Building Intersubjectivity

When collaborators/partners from different disciplines or occupations are brought into a project, it is important to develop an analysis strategy that accounts for differing viewpoints. As noted earlier in this book, cross-checking preliminary findings (which can be repeated in cycles) (Flinterman et al. 2001), also referred to as "analysis cycles" (Tenni, Smith & Boucher 2003), may be helpful. These strategies may involve one party taking responsibility for analysis/coding and then circulating the analyzed data to the other research partners for comment; and, continuous feedback loops and re-checking assumptions (Flinterman et al. 2001). Employing any of these strategies may result in the building of "intersubjectivity," which strengthens the validity and trustworthiness of the data. In a transdisciplinary project achieving intersubjectivity is significant because it implies that the various disciplinary perspectives came together to move beyond their individual disciplinary lenses and develop fully vetted and mutually agreed upon understandings.

Following Appropriate Methodological Principles

It is also important that you have followed the principles of the methodological strategies you are employing. This varies from project to project. For example, in a community-based research project it is important to follow the principles of CBR with respect to collaboration, sharing authority, creating the division of labor, bringing community members into the process in meaningful ways, using successful retention strategies, and building culturally sensitive definitions and understandings. In an arts-based research project it is important to consider the craft of the artistic mediums from which you are borrowing. Goals in an ABR study may include evocation, provocation and resonance. The "effectiveness" and "merit" of an ABR project might be linked to how well these principles have been realized. Further, "artistic merit" or the "aesthetics" of an arts-based representation may also be considered during evaluation. In this regard, "vigor" may be deemed as important, or more important, than traditional conceptions of "rigor" and the like (Sinner et al. 2006). Put differently, vigor may be viewed as resulting from rigor. When traditional quantitative or qualitative methods have been employed, it is important that their methodological principles are followed rigorously. For example, in a study employing quantitative questionnaires, norms regarding the development of the instrument (in order to achieve validity), pre-testing (in order to test the reliability of the instrument) and administration of the instrument (in order to maximize responses in ethical ways), and so forth, should be followed. Deviations from "standard" practice warrant explanation. In this vein disclosure of methodological decision-making can help build confidence in the research findings.

Representation and Dissemination of Findings

Transdisciplinary research should be evaluated largely in terms of its usefulness. I return to this issue later when reviewing the value of the project as an evaluative criterion; however, making the research useful, particularly beyond the academy, means taking issues of representation and dissemination seriously. In this regard, transdisciplinary research can be used to extend public scholarship. It is therefore vital to make serious attempts at reaching diverse audiences, the publics/groups we aim to serve. Depending on the nature of the project and the intended audiences, various strategies can be employed.

For example, the presentation of the data may follow an arts-based format. A dramatic performance could be staged as a way of seeking understanding across diversity, building empathy, sharing information, and creating resonance. Research findings could be presented in various formats at community venues such as community centers, local art galleries, local businesses or religious institutions. Research findings could also appear in local news, in the form of op-ed articles and the like, or on public radio broadcasts. Events for engaging the public can also be orchestrated, such as public lectures, information at street fairs, open houses at universities, and other creative methods for reaching broad audiences. Making use of new technologies for presentation styles and as venues for distribution may also be useful. For example, international websites may be created. When traditional research reports or articles are produced, researchers can consider publishing different versions of the study in different disciplinary publications in order to reach a broader cross-section of the research community.

Table 6.1 Summary of Evaluation Strategies

Strategy (Principle)	Practice
Responsiveness and Flexibility	Responsive or iterative methodology that prioritizes the research problem
Innovation and Creativity	Different disciplinary resources are used in service of the research problem
Intersubjectivity	Reflexive and collaborative analysis process
Methodological Principles	Principles of methodological strategies employed are appropriately followed
Representation and Dissemination	Research findings are made available to the public/relevant parties; creative formats and venues are utilized in order to assist in the dissemination, understandability and usefulness of the research findings among differently situated stakeholders

Evaluation Concepts

Holistic, Synergistic, Integrated Approaches

Although every project will be structured differently, the research strategy developed for a transdisciplinary project should involve a holistic approach to the research purpose and questions. Three concepts related to evaluating the holistic nature of the project are: 1) thoroughness, 2) congruence, and 3) explicitness (discussed shortly). In general, one can try to assess whether the scope of the project seems appropriate. Does the project consider "the whole"? This means that the research strategy should take into account as much of the issue or problem at hand as is researchable in a given study, and should consider the problem or issue from multiple vantage points or perspectives. The methods and samples selected should cover the topic effectively.

- Have the relevant bodies of disciplinary/interdisciplinary knowledge been brought in?
- Have key concepts been defined using multiple disciplinary and cultural lenses?
- Has a transdisciplinary orientation been consistently applied?
- Are the researchers open to new ways of seeing?
- Are the researchers open to building knowledge in different "shapes"?

Thoroughness

In addition to being explicit about what was done, why it was done, and what was found researchers must also make a case regarding the "*thoroughness*" of the project. Once readers have an understanding of how a project was conceived and carried out they will then judge whether or not a reasonable approach was used. Thoroughness speaks to the comprehensiveness of a study as well as the exhaustiveness of sampling, data collection and data presentation (Whittemore, Chase & Mandle 2001). As a part of this evaluation readers will use the concept of thoroughness, asking the following questions:

- Was a comprehensive and holistic approach to inquiry undertaken?
- Have the relevant bodies of literature (and disciplinary or practical expertise) been brought in and utilized both fully and effectively?

- Are the research questions thoroughly addressed by the data collection procedures? Are the research questions thoroughly answered? (Bear in mind that this is not always possible and need not undermine whatever progress has been made.)
- Is the sample appropriate?
  ▷ Is the sample the appropriate size for the project?
  ▷ Does the sample represent the population?
- In the case of a mixed methods or multi-method design, are the different phases of research connected to each other—do they inform each other?

Congruence

Another related evaluative concept is *congruence*. Congruence speaks to how the various components of the research project fit together.

- Is the project well conceived?
- Does the methodology make sense?

  Congruence should be evident between the research question, the methods, and the findings; between data collection and analysis; between the current study and previous studies; and between the findings and practice. (Whittemore et al. 2001, 532)

The issue of congruence harkens back to discussions earlier in this book about creating *integrated* and *synergistic* approaches to knowledge-building. All aspects of the research strategy should be clearly linked together. Moreover, cross-disciplinary resources and expertise should not be brought into a project following an additive model (where "more" is used for the sake of being "more"). Rather, these disciplinary wellsprings of knowledge should be connected in meaningful ways—synergistically.

In this regard Darbellay and colleagues (2000) suggest that "multi-disciplinary synergy" is a problem-solving tool. In order to operationalize this ideal they suggest researchers/research partners always look for where synergies between disciplines can be found or created (Darbellay et al. 2000). A practical strategy for doing this is to create inventories of what is "just beyond reach" of a particular discipline (Darbellay et al. 2000, xxiv).

Explicitness

Transdisciplinary research may be understood in terms of the evaluative concept "*explicitness*" (see Whittemore et al. 2001). Explicitness refers to whether or not a researcher has accounted for methodological strategies as well as the researcher's role in the project. There are several areas about which researchers can be explicit, including topic selection, research design choices, data collection procedures, data analysis, and interpretation procedures. If you as a researcher have been explicit in accounting for your methodological strategies as well as your own role in the project, a reader would be able to answer the following questions:

- How did the researcher and/or research partners come to the topic?
  - ▷ What is their interest, stake, or investment in the project?
  - ▷ What was their overall purpose or objective entering into the project?
  - ▷ What disciplinary and/or practical perspectives and experience did they bring to bear on the project?

Some of the issues that might be discussed in this regard are: relevant political commitments, social activist commitments or goals, personal connections to the topic, moral imperatives for researching the topic (such as solving a real-world problem or engaging the public in policy development), and other reasons for studying the topic.

- Are research design choices explicit?

There are several issues that might be reviewed with respect to research design. First, is the issue of the research purpose and research questions.

- What is the research purpose and what are the guiding research questions?
- Are these clearly stated?

An extension of the clarity and forthrightness of the research purpose statement and related questions has to do with the appropriateness of the purpose and questions. There are two main issues here.

- Does the formulation of the research purpose and research questions make sense?
  - ▷ Is there a congruence between the research purpose and the research questions? Will answering the research questions as they have been posed actually address the research purpose?

▷ Is the strategy useful and issue- or problem-centered?

▷ What is the value of conducting a project with this research purpose seeking to answer these research questions? Is this a worthwhile project?

Second, there is the issue of selecting particular data collection methods.

- Is it clear how the researcher or research partners came to select the method or methods strategy?

- Is the rationale for the use of this method, or more likely, combination of methods, provided or made clear?

- If hybrid or otherwise innovative methods have been employed, are their formulation and use made clear?

There should always be a tight fit between particular research objectives/questions and the method or methods selected to address those objectives/questions (Hesse-Biber & Leavy 2011). As transdisciplinary projects typically involve complex methods designs (e.g., mixed methods, multi-methods and hybrid methods designs) choices should be made explicit. This is also a part of creating a transdisciplinary research community and moving the transdisciplinary paradigm forward. Researchers will need to produce "records" of the strategies they used/developed, including their strengths and weaknesses. Sharing this kind of information is vital.

Third, there is the issue of sampling and recruiting appropriate participants.

- How were participants selected for the study?

- What is the overall makeup of the sample (for example how many participants were there, what were their major demographic features, and so forth)?

- How were participants recruited for participation in the study?

  ▷ Does this process seem reasonable and appropriate given the topic and goals of the study as well as any practical or pragmatic issues that came into play (such as funding, geographic location, sensitivity of the topic, limited populations relevant to the topic, and so forth)?

  ▷ What role did the community have in shaping recruitment strategies (if relevant)?

- What strategies were used to retain participants for the duration of the study?
  - ▷ How effective were those strategies?
  - ▷ Was there follow-up with participants after the study (if appropriate)?

In the case of collaborative research the same is true for the research team.

- How were stakeholders identified and invited into the process?
- Has the researcher or research partnership been explicit about their ethical practice?
  - ▷ For example, was informed consent obtained and was institutional review board approval obtained?
  - ▷ How have differences in standards for ethical practice been dealt with?
  - ▷ How was cultural sensitivity achieved, if relevant?

Fourth, there is the role of the literature review.

- How did the literature review help shape the research design process?
- How were relevant bodies of disciplinary literature and theories identified, understood and incorporated?

When writing up a project in an article or book format researchers should be explicit about the role of literature during all phases of the project, including research design, data interpretation, and representation.

After research design issues, you can look to the explicitness of data collection procedures.

- What did the data collection process entail?
- Can you plainly see how data were generated?
- Was training needed for team members (for example, on the workings of the CBO or on how to conduct quantitative or qualitative research or data analysis)?
- Were methodological principles followed?
- Was the process ethical?

The process of data analysis and interpretation should also be made clear.

- How were the data handled?

▷ How were the data coded or statistically analyzed?

▷ How were memo-notes generated?

- How were meanings built out of the coded or statistically analyzed data?
- What role did different researchers/stakeholders/community members have in this process?

  ▷ How were they trained?

  ▷ How did they negotiate and share their interpretations?

- What efforts have been made to put disciplinary perspectives into service of the interpretive process and/or to attempt to de-discipline?

In short, can you see the process by which the data were analyzed and interpreted?

Usefulness and Public Scholarship

I suggest that *usefulness* is a significant measure of success in transdisciplinary research projects. Questions to consider include:

- Is it a worthwhile project?
- Is the research topic significant/meaningful (which may mean, is the research topic significant in a local context)?
- Is there a moral, ethical or social justice imperative underscoring the project?
- Does the research address an identified need or set of needs?

  ▷ Whose needs?

Given that transdisciplinarity is employed in the service of issue- or problem-centered approaches to research, the usefulness of the process and/or findings in addressing the issue or problem is paramount. This is not to imply that the study must fully answer the research questions or "solve" the problem under investigation (more likely any given project, if successful, is a step towards a solution). Rather, one can ask:

- What is the value of the research? Or, how is this project of value?

  ▷ For what is it useful?

When thinking through the usefulness or value of a project one issue to consider is "the public good."

- Does the research serve an identifiable community, sector of the public, or the public at large?
- Has the research engaged the public on issues of import?
- Have the research findings been made available to the public the research claims to serve?
  - ▷ What mediums have been used to present the research findings to diverse audiences?
  - ▷ What venues have been used for the distribution of research findings?
  - ▷ Have representation and distribution choices been appropriate and effective?
    - ⊙ Have target audiences been reached?

In short, has the project been useful and has its value extended beyond the academy?

The preceding questions respond to contemporary concerns regarding the role of the academy/research community in addressing the fundamental issues and problems that are facing humanity. Transdisciplinarity is both a response to contemporary research needs as well as a response to perceived failures of the academic research community to build useful and meaningful knowledge. Ernst writes: "The universities should serve as incubators of novel concepts and act as radiating cultural centers that stimulate the discussion in the general public" (2008, 133). Transdisciplinary research practices which are grounded in responsive, ethically motivated, problem-based approaches to research have the potential to foster the kind of innovation and engagement that is needed to produce useful research.

Table 6.2 Summary of Evaluative Concepts

Evaluative Standards	Evaluative Concepts
Holistic, Synergistic and Integrative Approaches to Research	Thoroughness (comprehensive approach) Congruence (components of project fit together) Explicitness (research design, data collection and analysis procedures are made clear)
Usefulness and Public Scholarship	Project addresses an identified need, is useful, serves a public need Project findings have been made available to relevant stakeholders Social justice undercurrent

The Future of Transdisciplinarity: Building Bridges

In the United States the public is increasingly frustrated with a rigidly bipartisan political system in which nothing seems to get done because elected officials are too busy placating their party, too busy standing against the other party instead of solving real problems. Often, the whole political system seems to be at a standstill waiting for someone to cross the aisle. We can learn a lot from the failures of politicians to do their jobs because they are more focused on their political affiliations. Allegiance to party over people prevents progress; it prevents politicians from seeing and properly addressing problems that are all too real; it prevents them from taking their collective resources and putting them in service of the very people whom they are obliged to serve: the public.

So, too, has been the case in the academic community where it is clear that even with the best of intentions, borders and boundaries can greatly inhibit the kind of innovation and collaboration that are unquestionably necessary if we are to address our many pressing transdisciplinary needs. Society has big issues and problems to confront, and the research community needs to find ways to harness our collective expertise and resources in service of finding solutions. The problems facing societies did not develop within the artificial boundaries of any one discipline, nor will isolated disciplinary practices provide adequate (both broad and context-specific) solutions. For this we need to find ways to learn from each other and work together. There is a moral and ethical imperative underscoring the push for transdisciplinarity. Ernst warns that our world is "disintegrating" and academia is "obliged to fulfill a rescue mission" (2008, 132). Similarly, Nicole Morgan (2000) warns that the disciplinary structure of knowledge production creates competition and fails to produce a common purpose, and therefore there is an ethical mandate for developing transdisciplinarity.

In this regard Ernst pleads that there is an urgent need to break barriers in universities and create "combined projects" (2008, 127). After immersing myself in this emerging literature I suggest the fear that transdisciplinarity threatens disciplinarity is unfounded. While clearly transdisciplinarity and moreover truly problem-centered approaches to research force us to think about disciplinarity differently, they do not eliminate the benefits of disciplinary training and education which can be put into service of transdisciplinary efforts. In this regard Ernst writes: "Focusing is indispensible for understanding while widening the scope is needed for comprehension" (2008, 126). This implies that highly detailed disciplinary knowledge is a necessary part of the process but a transdisciplinary orientation is needed in order to be at the "frontier of science" (Ernst 2008, 126). In other words, disciplinarity can help us study the trees while transdisciplinarity can help us understand the forest.

Moving the Research Community Forward

Every new adjustment is a crisis in self-esteem.
—Eric Hoffer

The research community has a long history of fearing change and innovation. For example, challenges to positivism and the quantitative paradigm by qualitative researchers were met with great skepticism at best and continue to be a source of contention in the research community. Although Jones notes novelty can make people "uncomfortable" (2004) I think what innovation really does in these instances is to make people feel territorial (see also Klein 2000). Feeling threatened can cause the stark defense of borders and boundaries and the critique of new practices and perspectives. Evaluation is always one of the primary issues raised by those defending traditional research practices and standards. They raise the concern that if innovative techniques are used, rigor and quality will suffer and "anything will go." As evidenced in this book, which represents merely the tip of the iceberg of what is possible, there are many strategies that can lend credibility to even the most innovative projects. To go even further I suggest that new research practices have great potential to strengthen existing evaluative criteria and spawn the development of additional strategies for building confidence in our research endeavors. In this regard Morgan suggests that transdisciplinarity provides a pathway for building scientific standards which "have been in danger by the power of special interest lobbies, bureaucratic processes, and images" (2000, 41). She further suggests that the transdisciplinary research community needs to create an independent interdisciplinary international collegiate that negotiates and maintains transdisciplinary standards (Morgan 2000). While, following Russell and colleagues (2008), I have concerns that this level of institutionalization may have the unintended consequence of eventually hindering innovation, I think the suggestion speaks to the possibilities for the research community to come together, confront our fears, and continue to negotiate and renegotiate evaluative standards.

Beyond these kinds of fears regarding a lack of rigor and a threat to disciplinary authority, there are institutional structures in place and corresponding pragmatic concerns which can impede progress and result in what Klein elegantly refers to as "shortfalls of discovery" (2000, 52). The disciplinary structure of universities propels researchers on career tracks that promote disciplinary research and inhibit transdisciplinary innovation. There are three interrelated areas in which this is most evident: 1) promotion criteria, 2) the structure of academic publishing, and 3) funding.

The Structure of Academic Careers: Promotion, Publishing and Funding

The tenure system is a double-edge sword with respect to transdisciplinarity. Typically tenure and promotion criteria emphasize publishing within one's discipline, advancing one's discipline and developing a research agenda and publishing record in one area of expertise. This process fosters specialization and inhibits the qualities and practices needed for transdisciplinarity such as innovation, openness and creativity. Klein

(2000) notes that alternatively, institutional structures that value risk and innovation would carry great potential to promote transdisciplinarity. Additionally, tenure and promotion criteria favor single authored publications (often requiring them) which greatly limits collaborative projects, co-authorship and cross-disciplinary partnerships. Further, tenure and promotion timetables favor, and arguably implicitly require, an over emphasis on small-scale projects with limited foci that can be completed fairly quickly (see also Klein 2000).

Despite all of the challenges linked to tenure and promotion processes the tenure system also fosters the kind of academic freedom and innovation necessary to develop transdisciplinarity (Ernst 2008). Moreover, as interdisciplinary and multi-disciplinary programming, cross disciplinary learning communities, area studies, and integrated studies programs have all gained a meaningful presence in the structure of academic institutions (including the nature of academic life—teaching, research and service), these developments also pave the way for transdisciplinarity to grow. Further, I have to believe, to the core of my being, that if the research community is making strides towards addressing real-world issues and problems of import, academic institutions will find ways to support those efforts. Instead of waiting for institutions to change so that we can enact the transdisciplinarity that is sorely needed to meet the challenges of our time, interested researchers can develop problem-centered projects that draw on our vast repository of knowledge/resources/expertise, and in doing so will invariably promote corresponding changes in the structure of academic life.

Similar to the issues related to common tenure and promotion practices, the disciplinary structure of academic publishing poses major challenges to transdisciplinarity. I detail two aspects of this.

First, for tenure and promotion, or "career-building" purposes, researchers are often expected to publish in disciplinary publications, and are rewarded for doing so. Moreover, there is a hierarchy of first-tier journals and the like. Of course, publishing in these venues greatly limits 1) the subjects and scope of research likely to be undertaken, and 2) the audience for published research. With respect to the latter, the "disciplining" of readership greatly reduces the potential usefulness of academic scholarship and inhibits transdisciplinarity. Despite the proliferation of discipline-based publications we are seeing an increase in journals structured around topical areas and area studies, neither of which is bound by discipline. Further, I again believe that, notwithstanding the power of disciplinary lenses, when journal publishers, editors and reviewers encounter research that tackles topics of real-world significance or see trends towards transdisciplinarity, they will make the adjustments necessary to get the work out there.

The second major issue with respect to the structure of publishing centers on the form or "shape" of traditional research write-ups: the academic article/academic prose. While researchers often use the language of form or format to talk about the structure of research reports, I use the word "shape" (see Leavy 2009) which I will briefly explain. Many years ago my favorite musician (pianist and singer-songwriter) Tori Amos was interviewed by Charlie Rose. At the age of five Amos had been the youngest child accepted into the Peabody Conservatory but had her scholarship revoked at age 11 when she brought in a Beatles record and asked her teachers if the students could study that kind of music. She told Rose that her teachers just couldn't conceive of it because "it was in a different shape." The word "shape" speaks to the form of our work but also the way that the form *shapes* the content and how that content is received by audiences. Therefore, I think about representing research findings in terms of "shapes." In order to address different issues successfully and communicate effectively with diverse audiences, we need to be able to see in different *shapes* and to produce knowledge in different shapes. Moreover, by emphasizing the need to see and create research in different "shapes," I hope to highlight the ongoing role of the research community in *shaping* our knowledge-building and transmission practices.

For decades community-based research has demonstrated the need to think of the different and equally valid shapes that research findings may take, which have already been noted. In order to reach the communities we seek to serve, the principles of CBR have pushed the research community to open itself up to representational forms that can connect to the public. Likewise, arts-based practices which emphasize the representation of research findings in artistic mediums have also called attention to the form-content connection and influence the way many researchers think about issues of (re)presentation. Again, ABR principles encourage researchers to remain focused on the issue or problem at hand as well as the audiences that may benefit from the research. Therefore, ABR principles propel responsive, needs-based approaches to representation. Technological advances play a role in how the shapes of research are changing as inexpensive Internet-based forms of publication, digital photography, and other technological capabilities allow researchers to conceptualize representation in new ways. In short, transdisciplinarity is pushing the research community to "see" the outcomes of our research in relation to the problem at the center of a particular project and not ineffective or outdated norms.

Finally, there are issues of funding to consider. What kinds of research projects receive the funding needed in order to advance research agendas? This question is vital for both the individual researchers trying to build their careers as well as the research community as a collective. Often grants applications are structured in ways that favor disciplinary perspectives over transdisciplinary collaboration. For example, many internal grant opportunities in academic institutions as well as larger external funding sources require that researchers hold degrees in particular disciplines. Moreover, often review boards themselves are composed of members of particular disciplines with particular disciplinary lenses (including methodological assumptions and preferences). However, in an age of serious problems in dire need of attention even funding possibilities are expanding in order to assist researchers and research teams in addressing issues of import. For example, recently the National Institutes of Health (NIH) awarded $100 million over a five-year period and designated for ten different sites in a study aimed at better understanding and addressing disparities associated with cancer and heart disease. What is important to note is that the NIH awarded this funding to sociologist-led research teams. This indicates a willingness to consider integrated healthcare perspectives and/or holistic approaches to inequality in health and well-being which necessarily require transdisciplinary efforts. Again, I believe that if researchers put major issues and problems at the center of their work and bring in the needed expertise and resources to best address them, funding sources will find ways to support these efforts. Moreover, if we pool our disciplinary resources in service of transdisciplinary problem-solving we may find we have more support, not less. Either way, the challenges facing us can not wait. As Charles F. Kettering wrote: "My interest is in the future because I am going to spend the rest of my life there."

Notes

Chapter One

Transdisciplinarity: Disciplinary to Transdisciplinary Knowledge-Building

1. Alfred Schutz brought the term "life world" into sociology (Hadorn et al. 2008). Science had historically been detached from "practical life or the lifeworld" (Hadorn et al. 2008, 20).

Chapter Two

The Emergence of Transdisciplinary Research Practices: Conducting Social Research after the Social Justice Movements and in the Age of Globalization

1. This section on embodiment theory is adapted from Leavy (2009) *Method Meets Art: Arts-Based Research Practice*, Guilford Press (p. 183).

2. Traditionally a community is a group that 1) shares a geographic space, or 2) shares a common identity, experience or profession (for example, the medical community, the gay community, the Jewish community, cancer survivors). Sometimes a community is bound by both geography and a common identity, experience or profession (for example, jazz musicians in New Orleans, steel workers in Buffalo, the gay community in San Francisco) (see Shopes 2002). With the advent of the Internet we now have "virtual communities" whose sense of community may be transient or fleeting and may be based on short- or long-term interest in a topic, access to a site, and

so forth (for example, members of an on-line dating community, users of an on-line cancer survivor chat room) (see Leavy 2011).

3. In this regard, the field of "future studies" has rapidly developed over the last two decades in order to address the large, complex, and diffuse issues/problems that humanity is confronting (such as sustainability, population, unemployment, etc.) (see Masini 2000 for a discussion of future studies).

Chapter Three

Research Design: Issue- or Problem-Centered Approaches

1. Interestingly, Russell and colleagues (2008) warn that attempts to institutionalize flexibility and innovation in the research process may in fact inhibit those principles by stabilizing them. Once these features of transdisciplinarity are institutionalized there may be narrow or limiting definitions of what these terms mean. This presents the challenge of finding ways to encourage, foster and support transdisciplinary research in institutional contexts without unintentionally limiting its potential to address real-world issues and problems.

2. Sharlene Hesse-Biber and I also suggest a "spiral" approach to qualitative research in our book *The Practice of Qualitative Research, 2ⁿᵈ edition.* (Sage, 2011.)

3. Egon G. Guba and Yvonne S. Lincoln pioneered a model called "dialactic hermeneutics" which is similar to "analysis cycles." For a full discussion of "dialactic hermeneutics" see Guba and Lincoln *Fourth Generation Evaluation.* (Sage, 1989.)

4. I use the term "new" instead of "alternative" or "alternate" or "experimental" which often appear in the literature (and which I myself have used in the past) because I believe that these other terms may imply there is something less valid about these new forms of representation—that they aren't as valid as traditional or conventional formats.

Chapter Five

Arts-Based Research Practices: Designing Research That Is Useful for the Public

1. It is important to note that in the early history of scholarship the arts were not artificially severed from the sciences as evidenced in the earlier link between mathematics and poetry for example.

2. There are different terms that appear in the literature to describe arts-based research or related practices. For example, arts-based educational research (ABER), A/R/tography (A/R/T) and arts-informed inquiry to name a few.

3. "Theatre of the Oppressed" was developed by Augusto Boal as a means of challenging the dominant class.

References

Abbott, A. (2001). *Chaos of Disciplines*. Chicago: University of Chicago Press.

Agadala, K. (1991). "Households and Historical Change on Plantations in Kenya." In Masini, E. & Stratigos, S. (Eds.) *Women, Households and Change*, 205–241. Tokyo: United Nations University Press.

Anderson, B. (1991). *Imagines Communities: Reflections on the Origin and Spread of Nationalism* (rev. ed.). New York: Verso.

Anzaldua, G. (1987). *Borderlands/La Frontera: The New Mestiza* (2nd ed.). San Francisco: Aunt Lute Books.

Austin, W., Park, C., & Goble, E. (2008). From Interdisciplinary to Transdisciplinary Research: A Case Study. *Qualitative Health Research, 18*(4), 557–564.

Bailey, C. (1996). *A Guide to Field Research*. Thousand Oaks, CA: Pine Forge.

———. (2007). *A Guide to Qualitative Field Research*. Thousand Oaks, CA: Pine Forge.

Barone, T. (1990). "Using the Narrative Text as an Occasion for Conspiracy." In Eisner, E. W. & Peshkin, A. (Eds.) *Qualitative Inquiry in Education*, 305–326. New York: Teacher's College Press.

Berg, B. (2007). *Qualitative Research Methods for the Social Sciences*. New York: Pearson.

Berger, P. L., Berger, B., & Keller, H. (1973). *The Homeless Mind: Modernization and Consciousness*. New York: Random House.

Bergum, V. & Dossetor, J. (2005). *Relational Ethics: The Full Meaning of Respect.* Hagerstown, MD: University Publishing Group.

Bhabba, H. (1990). "The Third Space: Interview with Homi Bhabba." In Jonathon Rutherford (Ed.) *Identity: Community, Culture, Difference,* 207–222. London, UK: Routledge.

———. (1994). *The Location of Culture.* Oxford, UK: Routledge.

Boal, A. (1985). *Theatre of the Oppressed.* New York: Theatre Communications Group.

———. (1998). *Legislative Theatre: Using Performance to Make Politics.* London, UK: Routledge.

Bordo, S. (1989). "Anorexia Nervosa: Psychopathology as the Crystallization of Culture." In Diamone, I. & Quimby, L. (Eds.) *Feminism and Foucault: Reflections on Resistance,* 87–118. Boston: Northeastern University Press.

Boulding, E. (1991). "Prologue." In Masini, E. & Stratigos, S. (Eds.) *Women, Households and Change,* xi–xvi. Tokyo: United Nations University Press.

Bown, A. (2004). Mind the Gap. Unpublished play.

Brandao, C.A.L. (2007). Transdisciplinarity, Yesterday and Today. *Art Papers: Electronic Art and Animation Catalog-*Art Gallery. Atlanta: Art Papers.

Bruce, A., Lyall, C., Tait, J., & Williams, R. (2004). Interdisciplinary Integration in Europe: The Case of the Fifth Framework Programme. *Futures, 36,* 457–470.

Burger, P. & Kamber, R. (2003). Cognitive Integration in Transdisciplinary Science: Knowledge as a Key Notion. *Issues in Integrative Studies, 21,* 43–73.

Cameron, F. & Mengler, S. (2009). Complexity, Transdisciplinarity, and Museum Collections Documentation: Emergent Metaphors for a Complex World. *Journal of Material Culture, 14*(2), 189–218.

Carlsson, L. (2001). Non-Hierarchical Evaluation of Policy. *Evaluation, 6*(2), 201–216.

Chan, Z. C. Y. (2003). A Poem: Anorexia. *Qualitative Inquiry, 9*(6), 956–957.

Connor, L., Treloar, C., & Higginbotham, N. (2001). "How to Perform Transdisciplinary Research: Qualitative Study Designs and Methods." In Higginbotham, N., Albrecht, G., & Connor, L. (Eds.) *Health Social Science: A Transdisciplinary and Complexity Perspective,* 227–265. South Melbourne, Australia: Oxford University Press.

Creswell, J. W. (2003). *Research Design: Qualitative, Quantitative, and Mixed Methods Approaches* (2nd ed.). Thousand Oaks, CA: Sage.

Darbellay, I., Cockell, M., Billotte, J., & Waldvogel, F. (2008). "Introduction: For a World Knowledge Dialogue." In Darbellay, I., Cockell, M., Billotte, J., & Waldvogel, F. (Eds.) *A Vision of Transdisciplinarity: Laying Foundations for a World Knowledge Dialogue*, xvii–xxix. EPFL Press: distributed by CRC Press Switzerland.

Delgado, R. & Stefancic, J. (2001). *Critical Race Rheumy: An Introduction*. New York: New York University Press.

Denzin, N. (2005). "The Moral Activist Role of Critical Race Theory Scholarship." In Denzin, N. & Lincoln, Y. (Eds.) *The SAGE Handbook of Qualitative Research*, 279–302. Thousand Oaks, CA: Sage.

———. & Lincoln, Y. (2008). "Introduction: Critical Methodologies and Indigenous Inquiry." In Denzin, N., Lincoln, Y., & Tuhiwai Smith, L. (Eds.) *Handbook of Critical and Indigenous Methodologies*, 1–20. Thousand Oaks, CA: Sage.

Depres, C., Brais, N., & Auellan, S. (2004). Collaborative Planning for Retrofitting Suburbs: Transdisciplinary and Intersubjectivity in Action. *Futures, 36*, 471–486.

Derrida, J. (1966). "The Decentering Event in Social Thought." In Bass, A. (Trans.) *Writing the Difference*, 278–282. Chicago: University of Chicago Press.

———. (1997). *Deconstruction in a Nutshell: A Conversation with Jacques Derrida/Edited with a Commentary by John D. Caputo*. New York: Fordham University Press.

Diamond, D. (2004). Practicing Democracy. Unpublished play.

Eisner, E. (2002). *The Arts and the Creation of Mind*. New Haven, CT: Yale University Press.

Ernst, R. (2000). "Societal Responsibility of Universities, Wisdom and Foresight Leading to a Better World." In Somerville, M. A. & Rapport, D. J. (Eds.) *Transdisciplinarity: ReCreating Integrated Knowledge*, 121–136. Oxford, UK: E0LSS Publishers Co. Ltd.

Ernst, R. R. (2008). "Societal Responsibility of Universities. Wisdom and Foresight Leading to a Better World." In Darbellay, F., Cockell, M., Billotte, J., & Waldvogel, F. (Eds.) *A Vision of Transdisciplinarity: Laying Foundations for a World Knowledge Dialogue*, 121–135. Boca Raton, FL: CRC.

Faulkner, S. L. (2006). Reconstruction: LGBTQ and Jewish. *International and Intercultural Communication Annual, 29*, 95–120.

———. (2009). *Poetry as Method: Reporting Research through Verse*. Walnut Creek, CA: Left Coast.

Flinterman, J., Teclemariam-mesbah, R., Broerse, J. E., & Bunders, J. F. (2001). Transdisciplinarity: The New Challenge for Biomedical Research. *Bulletin of Science, Technology & Society, 21*(4), 253–266.

Foucault, M. (1976). "Power as Knowledge." In Hurley, R. (Trans.) *The History of Sexuality, Vol. 1: An Introduction*, 92–102. New York: Vintage Books.

Frisch, M. (1990). *A Shared Authority: Essays on the Craft and Meaning of Oral and Public History*. New York: State University of New York Press.

Frost, R. (1920). "The Road Not Taken." In Frost, R. (Ed.) *Mountain Interval*. New York: Henry Holt and Company.

Futures of Transdisciplinarity. (2004). *Futures, 36*(4), 397–403.

Gatson, S. N. (2003). On Being Amorphous: Autoethnography, Genealogy, and a Multiracial Indentity. *Qualitative Inquiry, 9* (1), 20–48.

Glenn, E. N. (2000). Creating a Caring Society. *Contemporary Sociology, 29*(1), 84–94.

Gibbons, M., Limoges, C., Nowotny, H., Schwartzman, S., Scott, T., & Trow, M. (1994). *The New Production of Knowledge: The Dynamics of Science and Research in Contemporary Societies*. London: Sage.

Giri, A. K. (2002). The Calling of a Creative Transdisciplinarity. *Futures, 34*(1), 103–115.

Gray, R. et al. (2003). Reactions of Health Professionals to a Research-Based Theatre Production. *Journal of Cancer Education, 18* (40), 223–229.

Greckhamer, T., Koro-ljungberg, M., Cilesiz, S., & Hayes, S. (2008). Demystifying Interdisciplinary Qualitative Research. *Qualitative Inquiry, 14*(2), 307–328.

Grosz, E. (1995). *Volatile Bodies: Toward a Corporeal Feminism*. Bloomington: Indiana University Press.

Haberli, B. & Grossenbacher-Mansuy, W. (1998). Transdisziplinaritat Zwischen Forderung Und Uberfonderung. Erkenntnisse aus dem spp Umwelt. *GAIA, 7*(3), 196–213.

Hadorn, G.H., Biber-Klemm, S., Grossenbacher-Mansuy, W., Hoffmann-Riem, H., Joye, D., Pohl, C., Wiesmann, U., & Zemp, E. (2008). "The Emergence of Transdisciplinarity as a Form of Research." In Hadorn, G.H., Hoffmann-Riem, H., Biber-Klemm, S., Grossenbacher-Mansuy,

W., Joye, D., Pohl, C., Wiesmann, U., & Zemp, E. (Eds.) *Handbook of Transdisciplinary Research,* 19–39. Springer Science.

Halpin, Z. (1989). Scientific Objectivity and the Concept of "The Other." *Women's Studies International Forum, 12*(3), 285–294.

Haraway, D. (1991). Situated Knowledges: The Science Question in Feminism and the Privilege of Partial Perspective. *Feminist Studies, 14,* 575–599.

Harvey, M.R., Mishler, E.G., Koenan, K., & Harney, P.A. (2000). In the Aftermath of Sexual Abuse: Making and Remaking Meaning in Narratives of Trauma and Recovery. *Narrative Inquiry, 10*(2), 291–311.

Herath, D. (2008). Development Discourse of the Globalists and Dependency Theorists: Do the Globalisation Theorists Rephrase and Reword the Central Concepts of the Dependency School? *Third World Quarterly,29*(4), 819–834.

Hershorn, K. (2005, May 5). Learning through Arts-Based Action Research: Creative Approaches to Destructive Dynamics in Our Schools and in Our World. Paper presented at the International Congress of Qualitative Inquiry.

Hesse-Biber, S. N. (2011). *Mixed Methods Research: Merging Theory with Practice.* New York: Guildford.

Hesse-Biber, S. N. & Leavy, P. (2006). *Emergent Methods in Social Research.* Thousand Oaks, CA: Sage.

———. (2007). *Feminist Research Practice: A Primer.* Thousand Oaks, CA: Sage.

———. (2008). "Pushing on the Methodological Boundaries: The Growing Need for Emergent Methods within and Across the Disciplines." In Hesse-Biber, S. & Leavy, P. (Eds.) *Handbook of Emergent Methods,*1–15. New York: Guilford.

———. (2011). *The Practice of Qualitative Research* (2nd ed.). Thousand Oaks, CA: Sage.

Hill-Collins, P. (1991). Black Feminist Thought in the Matrix of Domination. *Black Feminist Thought: Knowledge, Consciousness, and the Politics of Empowerment.* London: HarperCollins.

Hoffmann-Riem, H., Biber-Klemm, S., Grossenbacher-Mansuy, W., Hadorn, G.H., Joye, D., Pohl, C., Wiesmann, U., & Zemp, E. (2008). "Idea of the Handbook." In Hadorn, G.H., Hoffmann-Riem, H., Biber-Klemm, S., Grossenbacher-Mansuy, W., Joye, D., Pohl, C., Wiesmann, U., & Zemp, E. (Eds.) *Handbook of Transdisciplinary Research,* 3–17. Springer Science.

Holm, G. (2008). "Visual Research Methods: Where Are We and Where Are We Going?" In Hesse-Biber, S. & Leavy, P. (Eds.) *Handbook of Emergent Methods,* 325–341. New York: Guilford.

Horlick-Jones, T. & Sime, J. (2004). Living on the Border: Knowledge, Risk, and Transdisciplinarity. *Futures, 36,* 441–456.

Hunter, H., Lusardi, P., Zucker, D., Jacelon, C., & Chandler, G. (2002). Making Meaning: The Creative Component in Qualitative Research. *Qualitative Health and Research Journal, 12*(3), 388–389.

Irigaray, L. (1985). *This Sex Which is Not One.* Ithaca, NY: Cornell University Press.

Irwin, R. L. (2004). "A/r/tography: A Metonymic Metissage." In Irwin, R. L. & de Cosson, A. (Eds.) *A/r/tography: Rendering Self through Arts-Based Living Inquiry,* 27–40. Vancouver, BC: Pacific Educational.

Ismail, Z. (2008). "BRAINetwork: 'An Experiment in Transdisciplinarity.'" In Darbellay, F., Cockell, M., Billotte, J., & Waldvogel, F. (Eds.) *A Vision of Transdisciplinarity: Laying Foundations for a World Knowledge Dialogue,* 174–182. Boca Raton, FL: CRC.

Iyall Smith, K. E. (2008). "Hybrid Identities: Theoretical Examinations." In Iyall Smith, K. E. & Leavy, P. (Eds.) *Hybrid Identities: Theoretical and Empirical Examinations,* 3–11. Chicago: Haymarket Books.

———. & Leavy, P. (2008). *Hybrid Identities: Theoretical and Empirical Examinations (Studies in Critical Social Sciences).* Chicago: Haymarket Books.

Janesick, Valerie J. (2001). Intuition and Creativity: A Pas de Deux for Qualitative Researchers. *Qualitative Inquiry, 7*(5), 531–540.

Jantsch, E. (1972). *Interdisciplinarity: Problems of Teaching and Research in Universities.* Paris: OECD.

Johnson, R. (2001). Historical Returns: Transdisciplinarity, Culture Studies, and History. *European Journal of Cultural Studies, 4*(3), 261–288.

Jones, K. (2004). The Turn to a Narrative Knowing of Persons: One Method Explored. *Narrative Studies, 8*(1), 60–71.

———. (2006). A Biographic Researcher in Pursuit of an Aesthetic: The Use of Arts-Based (Re)presentations in 'Performative' Dissemination of Life Stories. *Qualitative Sociology Review, 2*(1).

Klein, J.T., Grossenbacher-Mansuy, W., Haberli, R., Bill, A., Scholz, R.W., & Welti, M. (Eds.). (2001). *Transdisciplinarity: Joint Problem Solving among Science, Technology, and Society*. Basel, Switzerland: Birkhauser Verlag.

Klein, J. T. (1990). *Interdisciplinarity: History, Theory & Practice*. Detroit: Wayne State University Press.

———. (2000). "Integration, Evaluation, and Disciplinarity." In Somerville, M. A. & Rapport, D. J. (Eds.) *Transdisciplinarity: ReCreating Integrated Knowledge*, 49–59. Oxford, UK: EOLSS Publishers Co. Ltd.

———. (2000). "Voices of Royaumont." In Somerville, M. A. & Rapport, D. J. (Eds.) *Transdisciplinarity: ReCreating Integrated Knowledge*, 3–12. Oxford, UK: EOLSS Publishers Co. Ltd.

———. (2004). Prospects for Transdisciplinarity. *Futures, 36*, 515–526.

———. et al. (Eds.). (2001). *Transdisciplinarity: Joint Problem Solving among Science, Technology, and Society*. Basel, Switzerland; Boston; Berlin: Birkhauser Verlag.

Krieger, N. (2005). "Introduction." In *Health Disparities and the Body Politic*, 5–9. Boston: Harvard School of Public Health.

Krimsky, S. (2000). "Transdisciplinarity for Problems at the Interstices of Disciplines." In Somerville, M. A. & Rapport, D. J. (Eds.) *Transdisciplinarity: ReCreating Integrated Knowledge*, 109–114. Oxford, UK: EOLSS Publishers Co. Ltd.

Kuhn, T. S. (1963). *The Structure of Scientific Revolutions*. Chicago: University of Chicago Press.

———. (1996). *The Structure of Scientific Revolutions* (3rd ed.). Chicago: University of Chicago Press.

Langellier, K. M. & Peterson, E. E. (2006). "Shifting Contexts in Personal Narrative Performance." In Madison, D. S. & Hamera, J. (Eds.) *The SAGE Handbook of Performance Studies*, 151–168. Thousand Oaks, CA: Sage.

Lasker, R. D., Weiss, E. S., & Miller, R. (2001). Partnership Synergy: A Practical Framework for Studying and Strengthening the Collaborative Advantage. *The Milbank Quarterly, 79*, 170–205.

Last, J. (2000). "Some Transdisciplinary Experiences." In Somerville, M.A. & Rapport, D.J. (Eds.) *Transdisciplinarity: ReCreating Integrated Knowledge*,193–202. Oxford, UK: EOLSS Publishers Co. Ltd.

Lawrence, R. J. (2004). Housing and Health: From Interdisciplinary Principles to Transdisciplinary. *Futures, 36*, 397–405.

———. & Depres, C. (2004). Futures of Transdisciplinarity. *Futures, 36*, 397–405.

Leavy, P. (2008). "An Introduction to Empirical Examinations of Hybritity." In Iyall Smith, K. & Leavy, P. (Eds.) *Hybrid Identities: Theoretical and Empirical Examinations*, 167–178. Chicago: Haymarket Books.

———. (2009). *Method Meets Art: Arts-Based Research Practices*. New York: Guilford.

———. (2010). Poetic Bodies: Female Body Image, Sexual Identity and Arts-Based Research. *LEARNing Landscapes, 4*(1), 175–188.

Lincoln, Y. & Guba, E. (2000). "The Only Generalization Is: There Is No Generalization." In Gomm, R., Hammersley, M., & Foster, P. (Eds.) *Case Study Method: Key Issues, Key Texts*, 27–44. London, UK: Sage.

Locsin, R. C. et al. (2003). Surviving Ebola: Understanding Experience through Artistic Expression. *International Nursing Review, 50*(3), 156–166.

Loftin, W. A., Barnett, S. K., Bunn, P. S., & Sullivan, P. (2005). Recruitment and Retention of Rural African Americans in Diabetes Research: Lesson Learned. *The Diabetes Educator, 31*(2), 251–259.

Lorber, J. (1993). "Believing Is Seeing: Biology as Ideology." In Weitz, R. (Ed.) *The Politics of Women's Bodies: Sexuality, Appearance, and Behavior*, 12–24. New York: Oxford University Press.

———. (2008). "Constructing Gender: The Dancer and the Dance." In Holstein, J. & Gubrium, J. (Eds.) *Handbook of Constructionist Research*, 531–544. New York: Guilford.

Lukehart, J. (1997). "Collaborative, Policy-Related Research in the Area of Fair Housing and Community Development." In Nyden, P., Figert, A., Shibley, M., & Burrows, D. (Eds.) *Building Community: Social Science in Action*, 47–51. Thousand Oaks, CA: Pine Forge.

Macdonald, R. (2000). "The Education Sector." In Somerville, M.A. & Rapport, D.J. (Eds.) *Transdisciplinarity: ReCreating Integrated Knowledge*, 241–244. Oxford, UK: EOLSS Publisher Co. Ltd.

Masini, E. B. (2000). "Transdisciplinarity, Futures Studies, and Empirical Research." In Somerville, M. A. & Rapport, D. J. (Eds.) *Transdisciplinarity: ReCreating Integrated Knowledge*, 117–124. Oxford, UK: EOLSS Publishers Co. Ltd.

———. (1991). "The Household, Gender, and Age Project." In Masini, E. & Stratigos, S. (Eds.) *Women, Households and Change*, 3–17 . Tokyo: United Nations University Press.

Max-Neef, M. A. (2005). Foundations of Transdisciplinarity. *Ecological Economics, 53*, 5–16.

McDonell, G. J. (2000). "Disciplines as Cultures: Toward Reflection and Understanding." In Somerville, M. A. & Rapport, D. J. (Eds.) *Transdisciplinarity: ReCreating Integrated Knowledge*, 25–37. Oxford, UK: EOLSS Publishers Co. Ltd.

McLeod, J. (1988). The Arts and Education. Paper presented at an international seminar cosponsored by the Fine Arts Council of the Alberta Teachers' Association and the University of Alberta Faculty of Education. Edmonton, Alberta, Canada.

McMichael, A. J. (2000). "Assessing the Success or Failure of Transdisciplinarity." In Somerville, M. A. & Rapport, D. J. (Eds.) *Transdisciplinarity: ReCreating Integrated Knowledge*, 218–220. Oxford, UK: EOLSS Publishers Co. Ltd.

———. (2000). "Doing Transdisciplinarity." In Somerville, M. A. & Rapport, D. J. (Eds.) *Transdisciplinarity: ReCreating Integrated Knowledge*, 15–19. Oxford, UK: EOLSS Publishers Co. Ltd.

McTeer, M. (2005). Leadership and Public Policy. *Policy, Politics, & Nursing Practice, 6*(1), 17–19.

Meade C. D., Menard, J. M., Luque, J. S., Martinez-Tyson, D., & Gwede, C. K. (2009). Creating Community-Academic Partnerships for Cancer Disparities Research and Health Promotion. *Health Promotion Practice, 12*(3), 456–462.

Merleau-Ponty, M. (1962). *Phenomenology of Perception*. Smith, C. (Trans.). London: Routledge and Kegan Paul.

Messerli, B. & Messerli, P. (2008). "From Local Projects in the Alps to Global Change Programmes in the Mountains of the World: Milestones in Transdisciplinary Research." In Hadorn, G. H. et al. (Eds.) *The Handbook of Transdisciplinary Research*, 43–62. Bern, Switzerland: Springer.

Mienczakowski, J. (1994). Syncing Out Loud: A Journey into Illness [Script]. Bisbane, Australia: Griffith University Reprographics.

———. (1995). The Theatre of Ethnography: The Reconstruction of Ethnography into Theatre with Emancipatory Potential. *Qualitative Inquiry, 1*(3), 360–375.

———, Smith, L., & Morgan, S. (2002). "Seeing Words—Hearing Feelings: Ethnodrama and the Performance of Data." In Bagley, C. & Cancienne, M. B. (Eds.) *Dancing the Data,* 90–104. New York: Peter Lang.

Miller, R. (1982). Varieties of Interdisciplinary Approaches in the Social Sciences. *Issues in Integrative Studies, 1,* 1–17.

Mittlestrass, J. (1992). Auf dem Weg Zur Transdisziplinaritat. *GAIA, 1*(5), 250.

———. (1996). *Enzyklopadie Philosophe und Wissenschaftstheorie, 4.* Stuttgart: Birkhauser.

Morgan, N. (2000). "Notions of Transdisciplinarity." In Somerville, M. A. & Rapport, D. J. (Eds.) *Transdisciplinarity: ReCreating Integrated Knowledge,* 38–41. Oxford, UK: EOLSS Publishers Co. Ltd.

Newell, W. H. (2000). "Transdisciplinarity Reconsidered." In Somerville, M. A. & Rapport, D. J. (Eds.) *Transdisciplinarity: ReCreating Integrated Knowledge,* 42–48. Oxford, UK: EOLSS Publishers Co. Ltd.

———. & Krimsky, S. (2000). "How Do We Research and Evaluate Transdisciplinarity?" In Somerville, M. A. (Ed.) *Transdisciplinarity: ReCreating Integrated Knowledge,* 230– 234. Oxford, UK: EOLSS Publishers Co. Ltd.

Nicolescu, B. (1996). *La Transdisciplinarite—Manifeste.* Monaco: Editions du Rocher.

———. (2002). *Manifesto of Transdisciplinarity.* Voss, K. (Trans.). New York : State University of New York Press.

Nisker, J. A. & Bergum, V. (1999). A Child on Her Mind. Canadian Bioethics Society Annual Conference. Edmonton, Alberta, Canada.

Nisker, J. (2008). "Healthy Policy Research and the Possibilities of Theater." In Knowles, J. G. & Cole, A. L. (Eds.) *Handbook of the Arts in Qualitative Research,* 613–623. Thousand Oaks, CA: Sage.

Nissani, M. (1995). Fruits, Salads, and Smoothies: A Working Definition of Interdisciplinarity. *Journal of Educational Thought, 29*(2), 121–128.

Norris, J. (2000). Drama as Research: Realizing the Potential of Drama in Education as a Research Methodology. *Youth Theatre Journal, 14,* 40–51.

———. (2009). *Playbuilding as Qualitative Research.* Walnut Creek, CA: Left Coast.

Perrig-Chiello, P. & Darbellay, F. (2002). "Inter-et transdisciplinarite: concepts et methods." In Perrig-Chiello, P. & Darbellay, F. (Eds.) Qu'est-ce-que l'interdisciplinarite? Les nouveaux defis de l'enseignment, 13–34. Lausanne, Switzerland: Editions Realites Sociales.

Picard, C. (2000). Patterns of Expanding Consciousness on Midlife Women. Nursing Science Quarterly, 13(2), 150–157.

Piko, B.F. & Kopp, M.S. (2008). "Behavioral Sciences in the Health Field: Integrating Natural and Social Sciences." In Hadorn, G.H., Hoffmann-Riem, H., Biber-Klemm, S., Grossenbacher-Mansuy, W., Joye, D., Pohl, C., Wiesmann, U., & Zemp, E. (Eds.) Handbook of Transdisciplinary Research, 305–314. Springer Science.

Pinto, R. M. (2009). Community Perspectives on Factors that Influence Collaboration in Public Health Research. Health Education and Behavior, 20, 1–18.

Pohl, C. (2005). Transdisciplinary Collaboration in Environmental Research. Futures, 37, 1159–1178.

———. & Hadorn, G. H. (2007). Principles for Designing Transdisciplinary Research. Zimmermann, A. B. (Trans.). Munich, Germany: Oekom Gesell F. Oekolog.

Poindexter, C.C. (2002). Research as Poetry: A Couple Experiences HIV. Qualitative Inquiry, 8, 707–714.

Porteous, J., Higginbotham, N., Freeman, S., & Connor, L. (2001). "Qualitative Case-Control and Case-Study Designs." In Higginbotham, N., Albrecht, G., & Connor, L. (Eds.) Health Social Science: A Transdisciplinary and Complexity Perspective, 304–339. South Melbourne, Australia: Oxford University Press.

ProClim, (1997). Footnote 14, cited in Pohl, C. & Hadorn, G.H. (2007) Principles for Designing Transdisciplinary Research, 71. Zimmermann, A. B. (Trans.). Munich, Germany: Oekom Gesell F. Oekolog.

Ramadier, J. (2004). Transdisciplinarity and Its Challenges: The Case of Urban Studies. Futures, 36, 423–439.

Riger, S. (1992). Epistemological Debates, Feminist Voices: Science, Social Values, and the Study of Women. American Psychologist, 47(6), 730–740.

Ritzer, G. (2008). Modern Sociological Theory (7th ed.). New York: McGraw-Hill. Robertson, R. (1996). "Globality, Globalization and Transdisciplinarity." In Friedman, J. (Ed.) Cultural Identity and Global Process, 127–132. London: Sage.

Russell, A. W., Wickson, F., & Carew, A. L. (2008). Transdisciplinarity: Context, Contradictions and Capacity. *Futures, 40,* 460–472.

Saarnivaara, M. (2003). Art as Inquiry: The Autopsy of an [Art] Experience. *Qualitative Inquiry, 9*(4), 580–602.

Saldana, J. (1999). Playwriting with Data: Ethnographic Performance Texts. *Youth Theatre Journal, 14,* 60–71.

Sandoval, C. (2000). *Methodology of the Oppressed.* St. Paul: University of Minnesota Press.

Scott, J. (1991). *Social Network Analysis: A Handbook.* London: Sage.

Simon, H. (1992). "Living in Interdisciplinary Space." In Szendberg, M. (Ed.) *Eminent Economists: Their Life Philosophies,* 261–269 . Cambridge, UK: Cambridge University Press.

Sinner, A., Leggo, C., Irwin, R., Gouzouasis, P., & Grauer, K., (2006). Arts-Based Education Research Dissertations: Reviewing the Practices of New Scholars. *Canadian Journal of Education, 29* (4), 1223–1270.

Snowber, C. (2002). "Bodydance: Enfleshing Soulful Inquiry through Improvisation." In Bagley, C. & Cancienne, M. B. (Eds.) *Dancing the Data,* 20–33. New York: Peter Lang.

Sprague, J. & Zimmerman, M. (1993). "Overcoming Dualisms: A Feminist Agenda for Sociological Method." In England, P. (Ed.) *Theory on Gender/ Feminism on Theory,* 255–279. New York: Aldine DeGruyter.

Spry, T. (2006). "Performing Autoethnography: An Embodied Methodological Praxis." In Hesse-Biber, S. & Leavy, P. (Eds.) *Emergent Methods in Social Research,*183–211. Thousand Oaks, CA: Sage.

Steinmetz, G. (2007). Transdisciplinarity as a Nonimperial Encounter: For an Open Sociology. *Thesis Eleven, 91,* 48–65.

Stoecker, R. (2005). *Research Methods for Community Change: A Project-Based Approach.* Thousand Oaks, CA: Sage.

———. (2008). Challenging Institutional Barriers to Community-Based Research. *Action Research, 6*(1), 49–67.

Strand, K., Cutforth, N., Stoecker, R., Marullo, S., & Donohue, P. (2003). *Community-Based Research and Higher Education: Principles and Practices.* San Francisco: Jossey-Bass.

Sumi, A. (2008). "New Initiatives of the University of Tokyo toward Establishing a Strategy for Sustainability through Knowledge Structuring and a Transdisciplinary Approach." In Darbellay, F., Cockell, M., Billotte, J.,

& Waldvogel, F. (Eds.) *A Vision of Transdisciplinarity: Laying Foundations for a World Knowledge Dialogue,* 167–172. Boca Raton, FL: CRC.

Tarlington, C. & Michaels, W. (1995). *Building Plays: Simple Playbuilding Techniques at Work.* Markham, ON, Canada: Pembroke.

Tenni, C., Smyth, A., & Boucher, C. (2003). The Researcher as Autobiographer: Analyzing Data Written about Oneself. *The Qualitative Report, 8*(1), 1–12.

Thomas, S. (2008). Art as "Connective Aesthetic": Creating Sites for Community Collaboration. *LEARNing Landscapes, 2*(1), 69–84.

Treloar, C. & Graham, I. D. (2003). Multidisciplinary Cross-National Studies: A Commentary on Issues of Collaboration, Methodology, Analysis, and Publication. *Qualitative Health Research, 13*(7), 924–932.

Van Manen, M. (2001). Transdisciplinarity and the New Production of Knowledge. *Qualitative Health Research, 11*(6), 850–852.

Vickers, M. H. (2002). Researchers as Storytellers: Writing on the Edge—and Without a Safety Net. *Qualitative Inquiry, 8*(5), 608–621.

Wallerstein, I. (2000). *The Essential Wallerstein.* New York: New Press.

Wang, C. (2005). "Photovoice: Social Change through Photography." http://www.photovoice.com/method/index.html.

Wedel, J. R., Shore, C., Feldman, G., & Lathrop, S. (2005). Toward an Anthropology of Public Policy. *The ANNALS of the American Academy of Political and Social Science, 600,* 30–49.

Whittemore, R., Chase, S. K., & Mandle, C. L. (2001). Validity in Qualitative Research. *Qualitative Research,11*(4), 522–532.

Wickson, F., Carew, A. L., & Russell, A. W. (2006). Transdisciplinary Research: Characteristics, Quandaries and Quality. *Futures, 38,* 1046–1059.

Worthen, W.B. (1998). Drama, Performativity, and Performance. *PMLA, 133* (5), 1093–1107.

Worthington, R. (2007). Community-Based Research and Technoscience Activism: A Report on the Living Knowledge 3 Conference. *Science as Culture, 16*(4), 475–480.

Index

About the Author

Patricia Leavy is Associate Professor of Sociology and the Founding Director of Gender Studies (2004–2008) at Stonehill College. She is the author of *Iconic Events: Media, Politics and Power in Retelling History* (Lexington Books, 2007); *Method Meets Art: Arts-Based Research Practice* (Guilford, 2009); *Oral History: Understanding Qualitative Research* (Oxford University Press, 2011); and the novel *Low-Fat Love* (Sense Publishers, 2011). She is coauthor of *Feminist Research Practice: A Primer* (Sage, 2007) and *The Practice of Qualitative Research* (Sage, 2005; 2011). She is the editor of the *Oxford Handbook of Qualitative Research* (forthcoming) and the co-editor of *Hybrid Identities: Theoretical and Empirical Examinations* (Brill, 2009); *Handbook of Emergent Methods* (Guilford, 2008); *Emergent Methods in Social Research* (Sage, 2006); and *Approaches to Qualitative Research: A Reader on Theory and Practice* (Oxford University Press, 2004). She is the editor for two book series: *Understanding Qualitative Research* (Oxford University Press) and *Social Fictions* (Sense Publishers). She is regularly quoted by the national and international news media for her expertise on gender, popular culture and other sociological topics and has appeared on national news programs such as CNN's Glenn Beck show and Lou Dobbs Tonight. The New England Sociological Association named Leavy the 2010 New England Sociologist of the Year. For more information please visit www.patricialeavy.com.